# COPING
# WITHIN THE
# ALCOHOLIC
# FAMILY

**Joseph F. Perez, Ph.D.**

Professor of Psychology
Westfield State College
Westfield, Massachusetts

**ACCELERATED DEVELOPMENT INC.**
Publishers

Muncie,                                    Indiana

# COPING WITHIN THE ALCOHOLIC FAMILY

Library of Congress Catalogue Number: 86-70658
International Standard Book Number: 0-915202-63-8

Cover Design: Colleen D. Ahern

Technical Development: Virginia Cooper
Tanya Dalton
Judy McWilliams
Sheila Sheward

Order additional copies from

**ACCELERATED DEVELOPMENT INC.**
**Publishers**
**3400 Kilgore Avenue, Muncie, Indiana 47304**
**Tel (317) 284-7511**

# DEDICATION

To the recovering alcoholic
whose strength and courage keep
me ever in awe.

# ACKNOWLEDGEMENTS

A book like this could not have been possible without the uniquely personal stories of many people. I am grateful for every contribution and am especially so to Jean Bitzas, Michael McCartney, Lynne Dunn, and Ann Remington.

Special thanks to my son Christopher. I found his readings and subsequent comments about the manuscript of inestimable value.

Last and most importantly, my thanks to Marilyn Mackusick for her typing and editing. She gave of her time and energy selflessly during the work week and on weekends too.

# PREFACE

The point of view of this book is that each family has its own personality. It is the collective product of all the members' personalities. Like its individual members, the family personality is dynamic, constantly changing, constantly growing. This is the healthy human way. A family which is not dynamic but static, regresses and becomes sick. The alcoholic family is static.

Among family members personalities become inextricably interwoven. Parents generally perceive their children as extensions of themselves and children in turn, identify with their parents. The health of each of the members, then, is a critical determinant for the family's health. Within the family context no one is alone in his/her ill health. This view of the family has led us to understand that if one member of the family is alcoholic the family is alcoholic.

This book will explain how crossed identifications between and among family members too often suck the non-drinking members into the dynamics of the alcoholic. The reader will come to see how the members' perception and way of relating become alcoholic, how their view of reality becomes distorted, and how their judgements, especially of what is normal, become impaired.

In the book are addressed the emotional deprivation in which the alcoholic family lives. Descriptions are given of how members learn to live in a climate which vacillates between an apathy bordering on catatonia and acute hostility.

Explanations will be provided on how in such a climate spouses learn to live with a host of unpredictabilities, i.e., will he come home tonight and be icily indifferent or will he beat me up? Will she be drunk when I get home and contradict and nag me all night about nothing? Tonight will he/she be mad, glad, or sad? What members of the alcoholic family have learned is that *to live with unpredictability is to live without security or love.* The lack of both of these will explain to the reader the reason for the most salient trait of the alcoholic family—a pitiably low self-esteem. As noted, parents generally perceive their children as extensions of themselves. Alcoholics perceive them as extensions of their own inferiority. And the children in turn, learn the lesson early and too well: they are like their parents—hapless, helpless, and hopeless.

The children of alcoholics are an important focus of this book. Steeped in broken promises, untruths, and dishonesties they grow up with a kaleidescope of neuroses. Chief among these are the inability to trust, a constant need for approval, unreliability, the inability to get close, a terror of evaluation, compulsive lying, and a generally frantic way of life.

Another major topic of this book are the family members who overlook the drinker's behavior and condition, who make excuses for it. They may even buy the alcoholic's booze. Such members find reward in taking care and doing for the alcoholic. These people are called *enablers*.

The most remarkable characteristic of enablers is that they are totally unaware of the role they play in abetting and maintaining the alcohlic's disease. Enablers suffer but they deny it and persevere in their enabling because they do not understand how and why their behavior promotes the family's alcoholism. Both the how and why are explained in this book to help enablers understand.

One of the best ways to understand the family afflicted by alcoholism is to analyse how its members communicate. In this book that is done. Thus, readers will learn how alcohol engenders distance and blocks closeness. They will come to see that elusiveness and double messages are common among members of the alcoholic family and that candor and self disclosure are rare.

If the effects of alcoholism are to debilitate and to disease in the two parent family, its effects are comparable, if not more intense, in the single parent family. Readers will see that single parent alcoholics leave their children few options. Unfortunate but true, the children of the single parent alcoholic too often learn early to become enablers and/or alcoholics.

The author had many in mind when he wrote this book. Recovering alcoholics will find it most helpful. From it they will glean and expand insight into their disease. Those who have been unwittingly and unwillingly cast into the role of enablers if motivated to do so, will learn how to therapeutically abdicate that role.

Finally, while the book is personally self-instructive it will prove to be far more profitable than that. As the reader will see, it was *not* intended only for those individuals and families who have been afflicted by alcoholism. Those who treat the afflicted also will profit from reading this book. Indeed, all those who seek to learn about the core dynamics of the alcoholic and the alcoholic family will find this book valuable.

Joseph F. Perez
Northampton, MA

# CONTENTS

# PART II   ALCOHOLIC PARENTS . . . . . . . . . . . . . . . 85

## Chapter 4   Common Denominators of Alcoholics . . . . . . . . . . . . . . . 87

## Chapter 5   Case Reports By Alcoholics . . . . . . . . . . . . . . . . . . . . . . . . 95

# PART III   CHILDREN OF ALCOHOLICS . . . . . . . . 115

## Chapter 6   Common Denominators in Children of Alcoholics . . . . . 117

## Chapter 7   Case Reports by Children of Alcoholics . . . . . . . . . . . . . . 127

# UNDERSTANDING THE PROGRESSION OF ALCOHOLISM

Alcoholism can infect a family insidiously, slowly, almost imperceptibly. The following stages are intended as a general guide to help family members recognize symptoms of the disease as it develops. Few alcoholic families progress step by step through the four stages as described, some families may touch on steps of the fourth stage within a few months of a member's becoming addicted while other families take decades to do so.

An awareness of the disease can facilitate an admission of its existence, the first step toward recovery. If nothing else then, this guide will help to both expand and confirm that awareness.

An important aspect is to understand and bear in mind that the progression outlined here is not an inevitable one. It can be, indeed has been, halted by millions. Finally, one can go a long way toward arresting and obviating the development of this progression if one follows the *Do's* and *Don'ts* outlined in the last two chapters of this book.

# STAGES

## STAGE I

1. Engages in regular social drinking. The individual is uncomfortable when there is no booze at a party or social event.

2. Seldom leaves a party not high.

3. Increases tolerance for alcohol. More alcohol is being brought into the house.

4. Begins to drink regularly two or more drinks before dinner, even when circumstances dictate that dinner be served late.

5. Resorts to alcohol whenever there is any conflict in the family.

6. When drinking in the family, does so more quickly and there is much more if it than when family life began.

## STAGE II

1. Occasional drinks at odd times during the day.

2. Begins sneak drinking. The increase in empty bottles and cans in trash noticeable.

3. Comes to dinner inebriated, i.e., with slurred speech.

4. Does not remember events, conversations during "cocktail hour."

5. Has arguments, and frequently has verbal and even physical abuse.

6. Becomes more quiet, distant, isolated.

7. Rarely participates in fun times without alcohol.

At this point the individual has become addicted. The family can be termed alcoholic.

## STAGE III

1. Increases alcohol consumption.

2. Receives speeding tickets and/or has auto accidents both minor and major.

3. Engages in more arguments, verbal and physical abuse, and/or violent acts.

4. Has problems in social and vocational areas and/or constantly complains about colleagues or work or people in general.

5. Spends more and more time alone and when he/she interacts with family does it resentfully.

6. Eats with family rarely.

7. Spends more and more time away from family, seeks out only drinking buddies or "betties" *or* begins to live a quasi hermit-like existence.

## STAGE IV

1. Presents what seems to be a constant state of anger and/or depression.

2. Loses job or has extensive problems in work.

3. Becomes unconcerned with grooming and cleanliness.

4. Develops acute medical problems, i.e., liver cirrhosis, kidney malfunction, respirator disease.

5. Enters hospital for alcoholism (not always of own choice).

6. Produces the family break-up by composite actions. Result may be divorce or death of alcoholic and/or enabler.


The following eleven chapters are designed to help non-drinking family members understand dynamics within and among families when one member is an alcoholic. The material will help non-drinking members better understand how they have been sucked into the alcoholic's dynamics, how they can break out of the web, and how they can help not only themselves but other family members.

# PART I

# THE

# ALCOHOLIC

# FAMILY

Chapter **1**

# DYNAMICS

During World War II raiding apple trees was a favorite past-time for us who grew up in Hartford's Italian south end. The best time to raid was around mid-August. That's when the apples were passing from tart to sweet. Besides, if we waited much longer than that, they'd be too big, too red, and we'd feel like we were *stealing* not raiding.

The best trees to raid belonged to old Mr. Johnson. Mr. Johnson was very different from any other man any of us knew. You see, Mr. Johnson spoke with a southern accent. The word was that he had escaped from a Georgia prison and was very mean tempered. I'd always been skeptical about the prison story. I wasn't about his mean temper.

Periodically we heard him beat his wife. Once I'd seen him corner, kick, and whale a little mongrel dog that had nosed into his garbage shed. Worse than all that, his house fronted on the school's backyard and when on occasion baseballs rolled into his yard he put on a cruel satisfied smile and pocketed them. Our resentment made it easy to rationalize raiding his four apple trees. In short, Mr. Johnson was an ideal enemy.

On a hot, humid day in August when Mr. Johnson should have been at work I was at the tippity-top of one of those trees nervously tossing green apples to my fellow raiders. Suddenly I heard the screen door slam open and shut; then the terrifying roar, "Gawdamn Yankee wops are at it again." My colleagues in crime were long gone when I scrambled and fell to the ground—at Johnson's feet.

The Tom Sawyer, Huck Finn-like tone of the escapade ended right there for me. For Mr. Johnson beat me like I'd heard him do to his wife, like I'd seen him do that mongrel dog. His punches gave me a black eye, his kicks a lot of welts on my side and derriere. Thank goodness for his wife's screams to stop, which probably kept him from killing me.

I told my parents I'd been in a fight. I had to. If my father had found out the why of my injuries, he *would* have killed me. Sicilian fathers never concerned themselves with understanding the *why* of their children's escapades. They reacted to them.

A few days later I met Mrs. Johnson in front of the A & P. She looked at my still bruised eye and murmured. "Sorry for you boy. That wasn't Ed the other day. It was the drink. Ed's not a bad man. He's just a drinking man, is all."

More than forty years have passed since the "Big Apple Raid". It's taken me that long to realize just how much meaning Alice Johnson's words really held about her and Ed.

What Alice told me in those few words (the only ones she ever exchanged with me) was that she and Ed made up an alcoholic family. Ed, she had told me, was the alcoholic and she his unwitting enabler.

I have learned that these are the main characters in the constant tragic drama played out on the stage of the alcoholic family. These characters and how they infect each other and the rest of the family with their dynamics will be the focus of this Part One.

# PERCEPTION

Perception is the cornerstone upon which we build our personality. How we perceive others determines how we interact with them. If we perceive positively, we tend to be open, receptive, sympathetic, and basically understanding. Quite apparently, such a perception engenders warmth and closeness and bodes only well for our interpersonal relations.

What we've learned about alcoholics, even those with the veneer of jolly-good-fellows, is that their perception is fundamentally negative. By and large *alcoholics perceive a threatening world filled with hostile people who want to manipulate and/or control them.* Such a perception explains their secretiveness, their apparent indifference and their seething hostility. It explains too, their constant need to distance themselves emotionally from others, including, indeed especially, their own families.

A most common aspect of the *alcoholics' perception is the notion that they are victims.* This sense of being a victim might be only latent in some alcoholics but it is a constant with virtually all of them. It is another explanation for the resentment and hostility of some, the submissiveness and surrender to the environment by others, and the general lack of energy to solve problems by mostly all of them.

The alcoholic's negative perception of reality has the unfortunate effect of distancing the family from others. Thus, alcoholic family members, drinkers and non-drinkers alike, tend not to "drop in" on other people. This tendency invariably has the desired effect—namely to discourage others from dropping in on them. Alcoholic families simply can not afford surprise visits for the obvious reason that such visits can be embarrassing—both for them and the visitor too. To avoid such embarrassments is precisely why members of the alcoholic family frequently and carefully arrange the specific hours when others are to telephone.

In sum, alcoholic families tend to be stand-offish. They seldom participate in activities with other families such as picnic outings or neighborhood parties. The children do not usually go on sleep-overs. Deprived of such common-place activities these same children become impaired in their ability to perceive what is and is not normal, what is and is not appropriate.

# CASE OF JIMMY

## (As Reported by Jimmy)

The following account given by Jimmy, a twenty year old young man exemplifies just how destructive alcoholic perception can be. It was edited from a tape.

*I was an only child but I never had much attention given me. My mother always complained about being cold and tired and she always looked it. I remember her always being huddled and haggard. My father only seemed to notice I was there when he wanted somebody to yell at. My grandfather who lived with us acted like he lived alone. He never came out of his room except to eat supper. In all the years I knew him, I don't think I exchanged fifty words with him. Childhood was lonely.*

*It's only now I'm beginning to realize how much I've been short-changed by life. Yeah, how much I've been shortchanged by my parents. Only now do I realize that my father and mother weren't much. I guess the best way to describe them is they've always been little. Yeah little people.*

*Biggest fact of my growing up was that my father was drunk prac-tically all the time. He was supposed to be a bricklayer. That's what he said, but he never went out to work. He had a bad back and he got some kind of pension from somewhere because of it. Anyways he was home all the time. So was my grandfather who was retired from the railroad. My mother worked as a seamstress. She used to leave the house when I did to go to school and she'd get home about five and make supper.*

*There were two kinds of supper in my house. The silent one—no one talked, or the yelling one. My father did the yelling. I realize now which kind of supper it was depended on how the booze had affected him that day. I preferred the silent one 'cause the yelling one made me scared. My stomach always did flip flops when my father yelled.*

*He'd complain real loud about how crooked everybody was. His favorite gripe was how nobody wanted to work. All anybody wanted, he used to scream at me, was to be on welfare. Maybe he felt guilty, I don't know. But my grandfather and my mother for sure never picked him up on the obvious.*

*What I've figured out is that my mother's a mouse. Scared. Terrified of him. And she doesn't have the backbone of a marshmallow. Sometimes he didn't go into his spiel about the screw-offs on welfare and would just pick on her. How lousy her cooking was, what a lousy house she kept and how "disgustingly" fat she'd become. (The word disgustingly was his word.) He usually finished this happy tirade with "And the cross of my life woman, was that I let you con me into getting married." She never answered him. Never said a word. Hard to have respect for a person like that—even if she is your mother.*

*My father spent most of the time in his work room down in the cellar. I was not allowed to go down there. "You'll hurt yourself. Power tools". (He talked like that—in half sentences.) He told me that when I was in grade school. He told me the same thing when I was in high school—and the same way "Power tools". I can't remember a single thing my father ever made with his power tools. Not only that but he never fixed anything either. When I was in second grade a pipe broke in the upstairs bathroom and the plumbers had to make a hole in the floor. Ten years later when I graduated from high school the hole was still there.*

*In grade school I took to going home with Tommy Marotta. I loved going to his house. People talked there and laughed too. After a while my father noticed and asked me why I was late coming home from school. I told him where I went. He yelled at me and finished with "Don't want you going there no more. Goddamn guinea wops. All crooks." Pretty soon I found out that he felt the same about the "dumb pollacks," the "dirty niggers" and "cheap kikes." It was all pretty simple. My father hated people.*

*I guess I always realized that 'cause as a little kid I never brought anybody home. I didn't dare. See, the people who lived in our district were Italian, Polish, Black, or Jewish.*

*During my high school years my mother got colder and more tired, my father spent his whole day in his workshop and my grandfather died. I spent all my days and my nights with my friends till graduation. My mother came to that. My father didn't.*

*I'm still living with them 'cause I can't afford an apartment. I've had a dozen jobs in the past two years. Always lose them for the same reason. Booze. See, I got my father's problem. The difference is I admit it.*

*Got nothing more to say.*

**Notations**

Three days after Jimmy made the tape he was admitted to the detoxification unit of a city hospital. It was the third time in less than two months.

Jimmy was born into the most emotionally deprived of families. His father's vacillation between fury and isolation combined with his mother's passive submissiveness have left him with few emotional strengths.

Perhaps in response to this emotional deprivation, to the fear that he would become like one or both of them, Jimmy unlike most children of alcoholics has developed and retained a remarkably accurate (albeit painful) perception of reality. Jimmy doesn't deny the madness of his family life. He sees things as they are, more importantly still, sees himself as he is—alcoholic and vulnerable.* And here lies Jimmy's hope. For realization of one's state is the first step and the pre-requisite to recovery for the alcoholic.

Also note that admission to the detoxification unit for some alcoholics can ironically also be a step toward health. For such alcoholics such an admission can be a cry for the help that they've learned they can not get at home. Jimmy qualifies as one of these alcoholics because he learned a long time ago that he could not obtain either help nor health at home. Consciously or unconsciously what he has come to recognize is that his help, as is true for millions of other alcoholics, must come from outside the family.

# NEEDS

Security, love, and self-esteem are basic psychological needs. How well they are met is as important for our emotional health as the food we

---

*As the reader will see this is indeed atypical.

ingest is for our bodies. In the alcoholic family these needs are met at best sporadically, often not at all.

## Security

A person's emotional security is premised upon a life filled with consistencies which are enhancing; upon the ability to predict with a high degree of accuracy what's going to happen. A person is reasonably secure if he/she lives in a home where people are dependable and reliable, where a promise made is a promise kept. In the alcoholic family undependability, unreliability, and broken promises all too often are the modus vivendi. Two consistencies exist in the alcoholic family. One is the dull routine of the alcoholic member(s). This centers around the buying, the drinking, and the inevitable sleeping off of the booze. The other consistency is that no one can depend upon the alcoholic member to participate in family activities. (Often non-drinkers in the family out of frustration, hostility, apathy, or whatever become similarly undependable). Promises come to be viewed as idle talk, at best nice to hear but not to be taken seriously. Spouses quickly learn to defend against hurt by taking that stance. *Children, on the other hand, are born believers and unfortunately take much longer to learn that they can't count on the alcoholic parent.* As adolescents and adults they become positively neurotic about promises. They seldom make them themselves and when they do they experience much anxiety about their ability to keep them. At the same time the promises of others are either suspect or anxiety-provoking.

## Love

Love is an indispensable need in healthful family living. It is the emotional glue which adheres members closely, one to the other. Families thrive on love for it enhances each member's personality and thereby the family's personality too. Indeed, a family's esprit de corps is founded upon the love generated in the family.

Love is often inconvenient and usually demands compromise and sacrifice. It always involves the expenditure of energy. What members of the alcoholic family learn over time is that *alcoholics will not be inconvenienced, and are incapable of compromise, sacrifice, or the expenditure of energy.* The alcoholic's one and only love, they learn ultimately, is booze.

The disease of alcoholism then, can not generate love between and among family members. It can and does generate rejection and indifference. *Alcoholism obviates love and any other enhancing emotion like acceptance, empathy, and respect.* Ordinarily, alcoholics do not reject other family members openly or obviously. No. Consciously or unconsciously alcoholics love deceitfully. In most alcoholics the ability to love and to communicate it over time are replaced by an apathetic-like indifference toward people in general and the family in particular.

Alcoholics can be, often are, good actors at being loving. This is especially true in the incipient stages of their drinking. In the end family members learn that the alcoholic can't love. The process of learning this is so terribly insidious for the family. For, in some, perhaps most alcoholics, the decline in the ability to love is slow, almost imperceptible. In others the decline is more merciful, for it is precipitous and blatant. Whatever the case, the decline in the ability to love is always destructive.

### Self-esteem

Self-esteem has to do with how worthy one feels about one-self. It is the critical determinant for one's behaviours. How a person talks, walks, and interacts with others is all a function of self-esteem. Motivation and consequent performance for whatever activity, be it tennis, work, or sex, are all influenced and mightily, by the quality of one's self-esteem. To a great extent if one thinks of self as good, he/she is more likely to perform well. If one thinks he/she is inadequate, then the person is more likely to perform inadequately.

The ingredients of self-esteem are security and love. The quality of one's self-esteem, then, is dependent upon how well the basic needs of security and love have been met. The prime source for the nurturance and development of these needs is precisely the family. As noted, within the alcoholic family these needs are met poorly, if at all.

Alcoholics have a low self-esteem and tend to view all other family members as being extensions of it. While this is truer for men than for women, it seems to be generally true for both. How devastating the impact of this view is upon the non-alcoholic spouse has been explained as the reason why so many men desert or divorce their alcoholic wives. (For a host of reasons mostly cultural, non-alcoholic wives tend to continue to live with their alcoholic husbands.)

Children are especially victimized by the negative perception of an alcoholic parent. A facetious but accurate explanation of such a parent's perception can be explained like this. "If I'm the big zero, then my kid's got to be a little zero." The victimization lies in the fact that the alcoholic parent *relates* to the child as if he/she is indeed a zero. The meanness and the hurtful effects of such perception was dramatically illustrated to this author several years ago when a fifty year old male client related with a twisted, bitter smile that he could not remember ever being addressed by his alcoholic father by name but only as, "Hey dumb-dumb."

## CASE OF JENNIFER
### (As Reported by Jennifer)

The author does not know, has never met Jennifer whose story you are about to read. The story was given to me on a tape by the friend of a friend. In order to preserve its authenticity, the tape was edited only for syntax and grammar. The story illustrates the tragic effects upon self-esteem when one is reared in an alcoholic home.

*I was brought up in an Irish Catholic neighborhood by Irish parents who were different. My mother and father didn't go to church. There might have been other fathers who didn't go to church but my mother was the only mother who didn't. But she made me go. At religious instruction the priest would come up to me, stare a little and then shake his head sadly and pat me on the head. At first I thought the obvious. It was because my mother didn't go to church. Then when he started his sermons about the joys of living in a big family with many brothers and sisters I figured it was because I was an only child. "Big families are happy," he'd roar, "because they are blessed by God". Small families, I concluded, had to be unhappy because they weren't blessed by God. The priest knew I was unhappy because I was an only child. In my child's mind that was the reason he paid me so much sympathetic attention.*

*I never knew why I was unhappy, but I guess I showed I was. My third grade teacher, Miss Cahill, used to ask me a lot why I always looked so sad.*

*Yes, I was unhappy growing up. I know now it was because as a child I never received what most kids take for granted, attention and love. I never got those from my mother. She couldn't have given me them if she wanted to. My mother was alcoholic.*

*She insisted that I come right home from school. I always did. (As a child I was very obedient.) And I didn't mind it. In fact I think I liked being told I had to come directly home because that way I didn't have to make up excuses about not being able to play if other kids asked me to. I didn't enjoy playing with other kids. They made me feel even more different, different in an ashamed, guilty sense. I know now it wasn't them who made me feel like that. It was me. I was a very unhappy child who came from a very unhappy home. Now here's the part that sounds crazy. I didn't know it was an unhappy home because I had nothing to compare it to. As a child I never visited other kids' homes.*

*Anyways I came right home after school and I was always very scared and very nervous coming home because I never knew how I'd find her—mad or sad. She was never glad. I don't remember a smile ever on her face. If it's possible, I guess I learned **not** to smile too. Maybe that's why Miss Cahill used to ask me why I was so sad all the time.*

*Mother never screamed or yelled like I heard some of the neighbor mothers do. She didn't think that was lady-like. She cried, whined, and nagged but always in a modulated voice.*

*My father was a mailman and very quiet. Supper and afterwards while they did the dishes (she washed, he dried) was nag time. She nagged him about money (we never had enough), about his mother and sister whom we never saw, about finishing a job he'd begun. (Dad put things off a lot. I think he did just to drive her crazy.) Anyway, supper was pick-pick-pick-on-dad-time. His role was to sop up her nagging. I think I got to hate him as much for taking it as I did her for doing it.*

*Like I said, my father was a very quiet man. He never talked, or at least he never began a conversation, not to my mother nor to me either. He'd go to bed within a half hour of the time the dishes were done. He watched T.V. I think. We each had our own. Three people. Three bedrooms. Three T.V.'s.*

*Dad died a few years ago just three months after he retired. The doctors said it was a stroke. Might have been. I've often wondered, in the past few years if nagging can cause strokes.*

*I spent my childhood watching T.V. I can't stand it today. When I do, I feel lonely. All that aloneness as a child, together with the fact that I never played with any kids, had its effect on me. It made me very shy. I blushed all the time. I blushed if the teacher asked me a question. I blushed if the teacher just looked at me. I just didn't want to be noticed. Once in the sixth grade the teacher assigned oral reports to be given in front of the class. I faked being sick the day I was supposed to give it and the two make up times. Finally the teacher let it go, probably because I was a very good student despite my shyness.*

*I remember once watching a woman's T.V. talk show and one of the women said all her childhood memories were "bathed in sunshine." Mine are all gloomy, filled with fear and loneliness.*

*My life began to change the summer I graduated from junior high school. Two things changed it. I suddenly realized that my mother was alcoholic and I learned that boys found me attractive.*

*I was sitting on the porch reading when I heard the garbage truck and the man emptying our barrels into the truck and then the comment, "What did I tell ya', Sam? Seven bottles of vodka, seven! Like that every week. One for every day. This guy's an alcoholic." Right then the realization struck! Her glass always in hand filled supposedly with orange or cranberry juice, sometimes colorless, was filled with vodka. Yes, Mr. Garbage Man, alcoholic. But it wasn't the guy. It was the gal. I still wonder why it took the sneering comment of a garbage man to make me realize it. That sneering comment made me realize other things too. Why I'd always felt different. Why I never wanted to play with other kids. Why I never wanted to go into other kids houses. Why it never entered my head to have them come to mine. Why the priest felt sorry for me. Sitting on that porch on that hot July morning, I suddenly knew everything. I cried for a long time. That cry and those sudden realizations took away my blinders. It was on that porch on that hot July morning that I decided that she wasn't going to influence my life any more. So much for the innocence of a fourteen year old.*

*I had noticed for along time that boys and men even, were looking at me. I developed faster then any of the girls I knew. My mother never talked to me about it. She just kept buying me bigger and bigger bras. The only comment she ever made to me was "You take after your father's side of the family, not mine." Those were the words. The tone was I should be ashamed. I wasn't and I wasn't because of T.V. All the messages there told me I should feel lucky. I believed T.V. more than I did my mother. It was a better friend.*

*Anyway the boys started coming around that summer. They'd sit on my porch and we'd talk under my mother's eye. She stood at the window sipping her Cape Codders, screwdrivers, or vodka straight. I thought she'd be mad or at least irritated to have kids I knew over. She wasn't. She began to look at me surprised, amazed maybe. The message was clear.*

*How come a weirdo like you has friends? Every once in a while she thought she had it figured out and would ask me "Jenny, Are you by any chance doing filthy things with those boys?" Sometimes she'd just come out and ask it. "Are you still a virgin?" My mother had a way with questions. Somehow they always came out like accusations.*

*Like I said my father was in bed pretty soon after the dishes. By eight-thirty, nine o'clock my mother was there too snoring off her bottle of vodka. The boys would joke about my **father's** snoring. I never told them who it was.*

*After a while the snoring became the signal to bring out the drink and drugs. The drink that summer was Southern Comfort. The drug was pot. We'd all pair off to the corners or outside on the grass behind the bushes. Gary was my first boyfriend. He wasn't a very good teacher or gentle either for that matter. But I was a very apt and willing pupil. We "went together" for about a week or so. (At fourteen lovers don't last terribly long.) Before school began again I'd had more lovers than a movie star and I'd learned all the different ways to do it.*

*I became very popular. And where only a few months before I had a terror of being noticed, now I revelled in it. My blushing days were gone forever.*

*The porch was too cold when winter came and since mother didn't want the kids in the house I started going out, right after the snoring began. I was careful to get home before midnight. She never caught me once.*

*My mad social and sexual whirl came to a screeching halt at the end of my junior year. I got pregnant (the word was "caught" in our neighborhood). All the terror, and loneliness of my childhood seemed to have been revived. It came down on me, enveloped me. I didn't know where to turn. I didn't have a single person in whom I could confide. All my so-called friends of the past couple of years, I realized, were strangers and superficial ones at that. I was utterly and miserably alone. In my whole life I had never felt good about myself. I had never felt like I was worth very much. Now I felt like a complete and total goose egg. You see, I didn't even know who the father was. The looks which I'd been getting from some of the girls in high school and which I hadn't noticed, I saw now. The snide, ugly humiliating sidewise glances sometimes with whispers and laughs as they looked at me suddenly were more painful than I could bear. I quit school. I'd lost interest long ago anyway. My parents could have cared less. My father had become more remote, my mother more alcoholic. She didn't even pretend anymore. She no longer colored her vodka with orange and cranberry juice. The liquid was always colorless.*

*I might have been terrified and bewildered but I knew one thing for sure. I was going to keep the baby. Single mothers were unknown in those days at least in our neighborhood. "Good" girls went off to have the baby and came back childless and resumed their "good" lives. Well I wasn't a "good" girl. I'd learned that a long time ago. At the same time I knew my life would be more pleasant if the baby had a father.*

*The day after I quit school I went to work in a local grocery store and that's where I met Kevin, the owner's son. He was ten years older than I and I could tell was really attracted. (I didn't show yet.) Kevin is not the kind of man that women look at twice. He's short and round. For once I played it cool and it was easy because even though he was older I could tell he'd had no experience with girls. I told him I was the kind of girl who had to have a wedding ring first. On the third date he gave me a diamond. We had sex and six weeks later we were married. The baby, a girl, was born exactly seven months later.*

*We had an apartment over the store and no one ever visited us, not even his father. (His mother was dead.) I had the feeling that his father suspected that the baby was not Kevin's. He never talked about it. Neither did Kevin for that matter. Right from the start I was miserable. He was critical of everything I did and never missed a chance to put me down—cooking, cleaning or how I took care of the baby.*

*Like me, he had no friends. I think he was looking to make some because he began to go out at night, to the corner bar. He started to come home drunk. That's when he became really abusive calling me a filthy slut and then demanded sex in his favorite way.*

*We've been married almost five years now. Kevin doesn't go out to drink anymore. He does it at home. He gets drunk every night in front of the T.V. I hate it because that is when he really nags and picks on me about everything. It's weird but I grew up to become like my father—henpecked. I guess that's why sometimes I feel like I married my mother!*

**Notations**

Listening to this story for the first time I was struck by Jennifer's apathetic view of life, by her virtual surrender to her circumstances. Jennifer feels like she's been victimized. Perhaps she has been. The only skill she acquired, namely manipulation by seduction, she learned via the adolescent peer group.

Unfortunate during her child years Jennifer wasn't encouraged to play and visit other children. If she had, she might have learned about the happier ways of others. If she had, her apathy might have become mitigated by a resentment even an anger for the sterile deprivation of her own life. Such an anger could have militated against identification with her parents' view that they were victims of life.

The life of Jennifer is the story of many young women. Its message is clear. **Seek Help!** Unfortunate but true, help for these women lies not in the nuclear family but in one or more of the many community support groups such as Alcoholism Anonymous. These organizations* are dedicated toward helping women raise their self-esteem, helping them learn from the misery of their lives, and helping them to change and to take charge of their lives. Such learning is crucial because only through such learning can they gain hope for themselves and,

---

*Found in the yellow pages of any phone directory.

most importantly, for their children. With such outside support they can learn to create an environment which mitigates the insidious effects of the alcoholism and even perhaps precipitates moments which enhance family members and the alcoholic included.

# DEFENSES

Sigmund Freud was the person who discovered defenses and first enlightened us about them. Defenses, he explained, are necessary to human living. Their prime functions are to protect us from emotional hurt and to feed our needs of security, love, and self-esteem. How well our defenses accomplish these objectives will determine how well we get along.

Defenses are selected unconsciously. Quite apparently, no one wakes up on a given morning and bawls out, "Hip, hip, hooray, today will be my rationalization day!" Although we are quite oblivious about our defenses, used properly and moderately, they increase our effectiveness.

Whether or not we use them properly and moderately is determined by how we perceive. As noted, alcoholics perceive in rigid and unhealthy terms. For some alcoholics the world is a hostile, threatening place filled with people who seek to manipulate. Other alcoholics take the view that they have been victimized by an uncaring, indifferent world. *Perceptions like these result in a defense system which precipitates distance and aloneness within the alcoholic family and between the family and others.*

Although defenses are described here individually they are considered this way for instructional purposes and for reasons of clarity. In actual fact defenses may merge and blend. More often than not they occur in clusters with one or more defenses working together and in support of one another, all to maintain the perception we have of ourselves and of others, be it healthy or be it alcoholic.

The nine defenses described here are the ones most commonly found among alcoholics and their families.

## Denial

*Denial is the prime defense of the alcoholic and of the alcoholic family.* When people deny they refuse to acknowledge a person, situation, or event the way it is actually. Thus, the drinking alcoholic by definition does not recognize that he/she is alcoholic. Nor do the family members. The family, alcoholic included, may talk about the individual(s) drinking, may nag about it, or may even joke about it. But they refuse to see the sickening effect which it has upon the drinker, upon the quality of family life, and upon relationships in the family. Like the ostrich who rids itself of threat by burying its head in the sand, the denial of the alcoholic family says, "If we don't see the alcohol, it doesn't exist." The family which is able to hold on to that denial is more easily able to maintain an even more important one namely, "We're not alcoholic".

## Rationalization

*The defense, rationalization, is a common support for denial.* When we rationalize we make excuses for, try to justify our feelings, attitudes, and behavior. A classic illustration is the alcoholic who denies his/her drinking problem and then rationalizes, "I never drink the hard stuff—only beer."

Rationalization is one defense that can be, frequently is, marginally conscious. Healthy people frequently know in their hearts when they are rationalizing. Alcoholics seldom do. The beer drinking alcoholic truly believes that getting drunk regularly on beer is a far cry from alcoholism, is simply not like getting drunk regularly on gin, vodka, or whiskey.

Family members out of a warped sense of loyalty and love invariably feed the alcoholic's rationalizations by accepting them. They do this in order to support the major, all important denial—no alcoholism exists in the family. *Rationalization, then, often becomes a most important supportive defense in the alcoholic family.* Family members make excuses both to each other and outsiders for the alcoholic's unavailability ("He's sleeping right now"), inappropriateness ("She was very tired when she said that"), or just plain rudeness ("It wasn't the real he!"). The excuses may be curt, or veneered with exaggeration, nonchalance, even with humor.

**Projection**

*Projection is the attribution of one's own ideas, feelings, or attitudes to other people.* As such, projection is a common defense of those personalities who perceive the world as being against them. For those alcoholics who hold that view projection is an integral part of their defense system.

When we project, we attribute to others the feelings, attitudes, and values which we harbor ourselves. Alcoholics, who perceive a world filled with hostile people and/or a world filled with people who are constantly trying to manipulate them, more often than not are themselves manipulators par excellence. This defense provides them with the perfect rationalization for their own manipulations.

Projection also explains much about the alcoholics whose behavior is characterized by passivity, whining, and submissiveness. These alcoholics perceive their lives as not being under their own control. Indeed, at some level many of them suspect that cosmic forces operate to control them. Projections such as these provide these alcoholics also with a perfect rationalization. In this case to surrender to their environment and, of course, to continue their drinking.

Projection is an especially infectious defense. Alcoholics who project engage in many secretive, non-communicative behaviors. (A favorite one is hiding bottles.) When asked candid, innocent questions they respond with partial or veiled answers. In short, they are something less than open. The effect invariably is to engender the projection defense upon the family members. After a while, spouse and children, too, start to look for glasses and bottles. They start to ask questions which are not so innocent or candid but veiled and hard. These behaviors in turn precipitate even more projections in the alcoholic. In sum, *the projection defense is a major reason alcoholic families find themselves caught up in much bizarre game playing.*

**Regression**

The games which alcoholic families play invariably produce much childish behavior. Behavior in an adult which is more commonly seen in babies and children is a function of the regression defense. Examples are pouting, temper tantrums, sulking, and crying, all to get one's own way.

Such behaviors, of course, are not the exclusive properties of the alcoholic family. Non-alcoholics can and do behave regressively. *Alcohol, however, compounds and intensifies regressive behaviors.* A sober person who finds it hard to hold his/her temper finds doing so when under the influence nearly impossible.

A common sickening effect of the regressive behaviors is that it generally begets feelings of guilt. Most alcoholics feel acutely the ranting and rages which they vent upon their families. Invariably when they try to make up for them, they overdo by making promises they don't want to make, i.e., to attend functions or to participate in activities they don't enjoy. Ironically and not uncommonly, the effect of these promises is to structure for more temper tantrums or other regressive behaviors.

### Fantasy

Fantasy is daydreaming. Its value for most people lies in the fact that it can provide an escape from boredom. Its especial value for healthy people is that it serves as a springboard for creativity. *Fantasy becomes unhealthy when the individual begins to find more reward in it than in the real world. Since the real world is not especially attractive to alcoholics, they invariably spend a disproportionate amount of their time in fantasy.* Men tend to fantasize about their masculinity and obtaining power and control over others. Women tend to fantasize about romance. The respective areas for both are usually where they feel the most acute deprivation and need.

*In alcoholic families where communication is minimal, fantasy occupies an important place in the lives of each member.* Fantasy becomes an especially crippling defense when the members begin to relate to each other and to other people in terms of the fantasies they have developed about them rather than as they actually are. The effect invariably for the members is even poorer communication among them and with others. This in turn, usually compounds the problem for the family members as it increases the time they spend in fantasy.

### Displacement

We displace when we vent upon innocent people the anger which situations, events, or other people engendered in us. The best that can be said about displacement is that it makes some people (usually those with little conscience) feel better. Drinking alcoholics are among these "some people". The vast majority of alcoholics, when in their sober moments, feel very guilty about the anger they displaced upon spouse and children when under the influence.

Displacement is an especially sickening defense because no one is ever made better by it, not the displacer, not the displacee. Quite apparently, one seldom learns anything valuable from being verbally or physically abused. Contrary to popular belief, the ventilation of anger does not usually clear the air either. More commonly, after displacement it hangs heavy with hurt, shame, and bewilderment.

Displacement can instill more hostility. Indeed, some displacers are just as angry when they're finished venting as they were prior to starting. Frequently, the venting process itself triggers off other items about which displacers feel they should be angry. Displacement can, often does, instill hostility in the one vented upon. Worse still, if this is a child, it teaches him/her that verbal or physical violence is a legitimate way of dealing with one's frustrations and hostility. In sum, displacement teaches nothing positive. This defense never enhances. Indeed, it only demeans.

In the alcoholic home displacements frequently have no specific source. Too often, no person, situation, or event made the displacer (alcoholic or not) mad. He/she was just mad. The ventilation was a response to an overflow of the constant, seething hostility with which many alcoholic families live. *In many alcoholic families the displacement comes to be seen as an integral and "normal" part of family life.* In some families it is expected because it becomes a way of communication. More than a few alcoholics have expressed to the author in therapy that there's nothing like a good fight to stay in touch!

## Avoidance

Avoidance is shunning. The shunned might be people, situations, events, or any activity that one finds threatening or even not appealing. It is a common defense among those who suffer with a low self-esteem and a low self-esteem is what is common among alcoholics.

The basic emotional rationale for this defense is, "If I don't try, I won't fail." The fact that nothing is accomplished or addressed is of minor concern to the alcoholic avoider.

For many alcoholics the avoidance defense can become a way of life and here precisely is the danger. Self-esteem is an active, dynamic aspect of the human condition. Self-esteem can not lie and remain in a state of suspended animation. Nothing human can. Self-esteem either grows healthfully or withers. It can not remain emotionally static. *The habitual use of avoidance by alcoholics is what sustains and prolongs the slow, insidious process of withering self-esteem.*

As the alcoholic's drinking increases, the avoidance often becomes generalized. Thus, where the avoidance initially may have been limited to not seeing people from work socially, the alcoholic may begin to avoid contact with anyone outside the family. In short, over time the avoider may become positively withdrawn. This is always a symptom of severe emotional distress.

The avoidance defense does not enhance children. Quite the opposite, it often deprives them. This is especially true if the parent alcoholic shuns children's play and activities and/or if the parent is threatened by crowds which are so often a part of children's entertainment, i.e., sports, movies, school activities, and so forth. Avoidances of this kind debilitate the parent-child relationship.

*The most unfortunate effect of avoidance is that it frequently turns the spouse into an enabler.* Like it or not, certain jobs have to be done in families. Bills have to be paid. Food has to be shopped for. The grass has to be mowed. Clothes have to be washed, ironed, and put away, and so forth, and so forth. Even in the incipient stages of their illness, alcoholics take little interest in these mundane family activities. As their disease becomes more acute their interest wanes further. Invariably, the spouse begins to take over more and more of those familial activities that were in the initial stages of marriage accomplished by the alcoholic. Some spouses do wake up to the fact the he/she is doing everything. Some never do. In both cases the way and how it all came about are a mystery.

# CASE OF ROBERT G.

The following account is an excerption from a psycho-diagnostic report which the author wrote over ten years ago when he consulted in a general psychiatric hospital. At that time this is where alcoholics were sent. The excerpt should help the reader to understand how psychological defenses become enmeshed one with the other and work to prolong and intensify the process of alcoholism.

**Name:** Robert G.

**Age:** 43

## Tests Administered

Wechsler Adult Intelligence Test, Object Sorting Test, Bender Gestalt, The Rorschach, and The Thematic Apperception Test

## Clinical Observations

Robert is about 5'9" tall, and weighs about 160 lbs. His face is lined and bears the scars of a rather severe adolescent acne. His sandy hair is short cropped and is thinning out.

Despite his quiet, non-assertive demeanor Robert seemed anxious about the testing. During the initial stages of the session he twice asked, "What happens if I screw up these tests?" After reassurance that the tests were not pass-fail types, he unsuccessfully tried to mask his anxiety with this facetiously tinged question: "Will I get put on some kind of torture rack, if I screw up?" Both questions together with the test findings indicate that like many alcoholics Robert is beset by much paranoia. At some level Robert feels that powerful elements are in his environment which can inflict cruel punishment upon him should he "screw up."

## Test Findings

The tests indicate that Robert's twenty year history of alcoholism has indeed taken its toll, both of his intellectual capacity and of his emotional wherewithal. He was tested last, twelve years ago on his second admission for alcoholism. At that time the psychologist described his thinking as syntaxical, intellectualized, and cognitively brilliant. His I.Q. Full Scale score was 135, placing him in the very superior ranges of intelligence and in the upper one percent of the national population.

Robert's thinking is not syntaxical or intellectualized anymore. It is concretistic. He has difficulty in making definitions and seeing similarities between words. Ideas confuse him. This general deterioration is reflected in his current I.Q. 86, which places him in the dull normal range of intelligence and in the lower quarter of the national population.

Robert's social and interpersonal judgement are acutely deficient and can be characterized as inappropriate, confused, and childlike. His intellectual degeneration is complemented by a severely impaired perception of reality. Stated simply, Robert often is not able to see or understand what is demanded of him. The defense system which Robert has developed in response to his distorted view of his world is almost textbook-like and classically alcoholic. It goes a long way toward explaining why and how Robert has maintained his chronic addiction.

The prime two defenses in his repertoire are denial and projection. Via the first he is able to maintain the illusion that he is not alcoholic despite the fact that he has been admitted to this hospital sixteen times over the past four years for acute intoxication! On these prior admissions when I myself confronted him about his addiction he would smile sheepishly and allow that maybe he'd had one or two more than he should have. He no longer smiles sheepishly. Indeed, no longer does he even react to confrontational questions about his alcoholism. Now Robert just shrugs.

The shrugs are due not only to organic impairment but just as importantly, to the projection defense. Robert's illness has progressed to the point where he believes that he is controlled by what he calls, "The Force". The Force, he will tell you after much prodding, is everywhere and anywhere. Robert believes that once it enters you, you are possessed and "forced" to do its bidding. The force enters people indiscriminately, he explains slowly. (Robert gives the impression he's still figuring out details.) Some people are never entered by the Force. Some are. He is one of the unlucky ones. As Robert sees it, he has no alternative but to live under the dictates of the Force.

The fantasy defense is of course the source for this elaborate projection. The bizarre quality of it all illustrates how atrophied Robert's contact with the real world has become.

At times Robert turns to the regression defense to support his childlike credence in the Force. Thus, at the last group therapy session he pouted and sulked when his peers ridiculed him about his avowed belief in the Force. (In a weak moment he apparently confided his belief to a member of the group.)

I'm convinced that Robert will continue to adhere and rigidly to this projection. This intricate emotional concoction provides wonderful rationalizations for him. Thus, it helps to alleviate any residual conflict he might have about drinking himself into a stupor when presented with the opportunity. (The Force is in control of him. He's not.) Also, this projection assuages and provides marvelous excuses for any guilt which he might feel when he comes out of these same stupors. (Not my fault the Force made me do it.)

The acute decline in Robert's competence with words for a time resulted in his almost constant use of displacement. (This was especially true on his last three admission stays.) Frustrated in his inability to defend himself verbally with his age peers, he began to pick on those older, smaller, and less able than he. This defense has not been especially evident on this current admission. It seems to have been replaced by avoidance and withdrawal. During most of the testing session Robert held his head down, just as he does in group session. Worse, a general withdrawal from self seems to be evident. This last is manifested not only in his detached non-assertive manner but in his unkempt appearance, ill fitting clothes, and non-existent grooming.

**Diagnostic Impression**

Dementia associated with alcoholism—severe

Joseph F. Perez Ph.D.
Consulting Clinical Psychologist

**Epilogue To Robert's Story**

Robert died three years ago. He was a month shy of his fifty-first birthday. He died alone, in the hallway of an abandoned tenemant in Springfield, Massachusetts on the 15th of January. He froze to death.

I remembered that he had had a family—a wife, Mary, and a couple of kids. I had met her on one of his earliest admissions. I remembered seeing him and his wife in couples therapy over a period of several months. Through colleagues at the hospital where I had consulted I learned that she had divorced Robert a dozen years ago, had remarried, and was living close by. I contacted her, explained that I was writing a book and that I thought Robert's story exemplified some of the alcoholic dynamics that I was trying to explain. She agreed to see me. The following is edited and taken from a tape.

**Perez:** *What do you remember about the first years with Robert?*

**Mary:** *What I remember is that everything was great. We got married when Bob was in college. He graduated, got his C.P.A., and got a terrific job. If he had a problem, I never saw it. In fact I used to drink with him. On occasion I got feeling pretty good myself with him. During the first three and four years he worked at the same job and I had the two kids. Great. The first years were great!*

**Perez:** *When did the drink become a problem?*

**Mary:** *I'm not sure. I didn't see it for years. I probably was as crazy as he was. David my oldest, was going into junior high school when I had my first inklings that there might be a problem. I was cleaning in Bob's study. He had told me not to do that. But it was becoming such a pig-sty. I couldn't stand it anymore. I decided to dust, pick up a little. Behind the desk, which was kitty corner to the wall, I found a shopping bag full of empty liquor bottles.*

**Perez:** *What did you do?*

**Mary:** *I threw them away. I didn't want the boys to see them.*

**Perez:** *Did you talk to him?*

**Mary:** *I did that. He pooh-poohed away my concern. I guess I wanted him to. Bob was a lot smarter than I was. He could make everything sound right especially when it was awful. I realize now a lot of that was because I wanted him to. Like I said, I was as crazy as he was.*

**Perez:** *Did you find any more bottles?*

**Mary:** *Not for a long time. Maybe because I didn't want to. Maybe because he got better at sneaking them. Maybe both. I'm not sure. He was drinking a lot. He always got drunk at a party. Crazy but I didn't notice that for a long time either because a lot of people got drunk or at least I thought they did. It was only when a friend pointed out to me that Bob preferred to drink than eat, that he was always the last one to eat at the buffets, that I began to become really concerned. I began to look to see if it was true. It was. At the next party he didn't eat at all. I had to drive home. I couldn't get him to bed. He slept in the car all night. The next day we had it out.* (Mary chuckled) *Seems like we had it out regularly.*

**Perez:** *What do you mean by 'had it out'?*

**Mary:** *I ranted and he just smiled, nodded and promised.*

**Perez:** *And nothing happened.*

**Mary:** *Until the first hospital admission. We started seeing you after that. Things were almost normal while we saw you.*

**Perez:** *Then they got worse again.*

**Mary:** *Worse. God! I found myself nagging him to take showers. He literally began to smell! We stopped going out. He began to be admitted to the hospital regularly. Did you know he did it from bars?*

**Perez:** *What do you mean from bars?*

**Mary:** *He had taxi drivers take him to the hospital and leave him on the front steps. They did and he'd get admitted. He learned all the tricks. He did that just so he wouldn't have to face me. He turned me into a nagging bitch.*

**Perez:** *You left him.*

**Mary:** *Right after he lost his third job. The kids were in high school, past the formative years maybe, but still impressionable. Anyway I left him and went to live with my mother.*

**Perez:** *Mary, did he ever abuse you or the kids?*

**Mary:** *No. Never. Not before he drank, not during. Never. Bob was not a violent man. In fact without alcohol he would have been a saint.*

**Perez:** *Did he ever talk or mention the "Force" to you?*

**Mary:** *The Force. I don't think so-o-o. Oh yes. Yes. (Smiling) He had a story he told the kids when they were small at bed time all about the "Cosmic Force". He told it in installments. It was all about invisible aliens from outer space. I swear the story went on for about a year. Why do you ask? How did you know about it? I'd forgotten it.*

**Perez:** *Not important anymore.*

**Comments:** At this point I thanked her. She started to leave, than at the door handed me a note written by Robert which said, "Maybe this will make up a little for the bad times with me. Maybe it will help celebrate your good times now."

**Perez:** *What does it mean?*

**Comments:** Mary gave me a sad smile. I thought she was going to cry. She didn't.

**Mary:** *Bob was dead for almost three months before I knew. The veterans agent brought me his insurance check with this note. He had promised Bob he'd do that. Bob kept me as his beneficiary. He found out my new married name and changed it to that. I'd forgotten about the insurance. I was sure he had let it lapse like he'd let his whole life lapse. He didn't. I loved Bob when I married him. I didn't at the end. I cry now and again for what he might have been. For what we might have been together. (Mary shrugged.) What a waste. (She left.)*

### Counselor's Notes

What we learn from Mary's story is that it is far better to face the reality of alcoholism at its first inkling than do so later. She should never have thrown the empty bottles away. When she did that she was telling Bob that his secretive drinking was perfectly okay or at least that he could drink alcoholically with impunity.

Mary's basic motive was a common one. Via the denial defense Mary sought to maintain a nice respectable veneer to family life. When she did that she unwittingly communicated to Bob that she could and would adjust to an alcoholic way of life. In denying Bob's alcoholism Mary contributed to the creation of an alcoholic family as much as he did.

What should Mary have done? Once she realized that Bob was alcoholic she should have learned all that she could about the disease. In the process she would have strengthened herself and come to know her husband better and thereby come to realize how poor their relationship actually was. The reality was that Bob had become alcoholic without her being aware of it!

By strengthening herself then, she would have strengthened their relationship, their marriage. Under such circumstances the counseling would have been more profitable and doubtlessly would have continued longer.

What she should not have done was to scold, argue, and moralize. Such behavior probably fueled Bob's drinking. By taking him back after each hospital admission without demanding or even expecting any change in his behavior she undoubtedly let Bob think that she accepted his promises to stop drinking. In doing that she gave him the impression (common among alcoholics) that a promise made is the same as a promise kept. Crazy but true, all too often that's all an alcoholic needs to continue drinking—to make a promise to stop!

In putting up with his broken promises she let him know that he didn't have to be responsible and in putting up with his irresponsibility Mary communicated a passivity and submissiveness which told Bob and her children too, that there were no limits to the abuse that she would and could absorb. Quite obviously, such behavior effects a lack of respect by all concerned including self.

The reader might get the impression from this discussion that the causes of Bob's alcoholism resided in Mary's behavior.

Not true! Mary's behaviors were only a *response* to Bob's, they didn't *motivate* his drinking. Even if Mary had followed each of these shoulds and should nots impeccably Bob might have persevered in his drinking. It was his choice to do so. He did it! Quite simply, no one is responsible for another's alcoholism.

Chapter **2**

# THE ENABLER

Just as no two alcoholics are alike neither are two enablers alike. At the same time there are certain common denominators in the personalities of enablers which facilitate the alcoholic process in family members(s). Enablers are disposed to be

    1. overprotective,

    2. compulsive, and

    3. worriers.

# OVERPROTECTIVE

*Overprotective* enablers, like overprotective parents, are not loving but rejecting. The overprotective parent does not view the child as a separate and independent human being, does not understand that the child's emotional health, growth, and maturity lie in making his/her own choices and decisions, in being responsible for own behavior. In short, the overprotective parent perceives the child (regardless of age) as basically helpless and inept which is more often than not the parent's unconscious self-view (projection defense). Both perception and defense are precisely those used by this type enabler toward the alcoholic. The overprotective enabler serves as a buffer between the alcoholic and the rest of the world. The rest of the world may even include the rest of the family. Thus the enabler may lie, explain, defend the alcoholic to children, parents, and outsiders. *Most enablers in their zeal to protect, defend, and explain the alcoholic's behavior do not see that they are actually feeding and nurturing irresponsibility and immaturity.* Indeed their overprotectiveness creates a womb-like world for the alcoholic's mundane physical needs and insulates him/her from the normal, usual demands and anxieties of daily living. The alcoholic is excused from family chores, from most social obligations, sometimes even from holding a job. Such an alcoholic seems to be excused from life. Such a cocoon-like existence maintains the alcoholism and thereby accelerates the physical, intellectual, and emotional deterioration.

Overprotective enablers are people who need to control and manipulate. In the domineering type enabler this need is easy to see in the arbitrariness, in the fiats, and so forth. In the submissive or more differential type of enabler this need is more covert but just as, if not more, demeaning. In these latter types it usually can be seen in the intense inordinate interest which they take in their alcoholics' lives, in what they eat, whom they see, where they go, where they are at any moment. Via this interest, complemented usually with the disposition to do, do, do for the alcoholic, the enabler is able to control the alcoholic's meals, social life, indeed virtually all of the alcoholic's movements. Overprotective enablers who find reward in achieving such control of another's life seem to fill an acute need for personal security.

This need for personal security is a prime motivator for overprotective enablers. Simply, they can best be understood as being concerned primarily with their own selves. Why? Because their intent, conscious or unconscious, is to turn the alcoholic into an overdevoted and obligated companion. This is especially true of those who persevere in their enabling even after they become aware of it. These enablers seem to exist with a latent but constant anxiety that in the end they will be left alone. The irony is that more often than not their enabling accomplishes just that since enabling does nothing to engender loyalty.

# COMPULSIVE

Enablers tend to be *compulsive*. Their constant and most important mission, among their many, is to solve any and all family problems. They set up and implement schedules, not only their own but those of the rest of the family members, alcoholic or not. They tend to the myriad of family chores that need tending. If they can not for whatever reason deal with a minor task themselves, they will bully or manipulate another family member into doing it. Then they will supervise to see that whatever was to be done was done to their satisfaction—meaning in letter perfect fashion.

This concern with letter perfection distinguises the compulsive enabler from the normally efficient person. Some enablers acquire this trait very early in their relationship with the alcoholic, others acquire it late, in still others it seems to be positively congenital. Regardless at what point they incorporate this trait into their personalities, it is the one which is most apparent and the one which precipitates arguments, fights, and stresses of all kinds in the family. It is the trait which alienates children especially. Usually because of this trait children come to sympathize with the alcoholic, turn to him/her for closeness. Indeed, *the enabler's compulsive ways may well be a prime reason that so many children of alcoholics become themselves alcoholic.* Many come to conclude that it's better to be a relaxed drunk than a frantic, compulsive enabler.

Why are most enablers compulsive? The answer seems to lie in the alcoholic's withdrawal from the family. The enabler's compulsiveness in most cases can be understood as the response to that withdrawal. They feel that their compulsive ways bring order and sanity to the chaos and indifference which alcoholism brings into the family.

Compulsiveness in the enabler is a response to something else too. Please note that compulsive people are usually people in constant motion —physically, intellectually, and/or emotionally. They're always doing something. Now, such activity has a most important benefit to alcoholic enablers as it distracts them from seeing the alcoholic's drinking. Such activity has another important benefit for enablers in that it prevents them from focusing on their inner selves and on how they continue to contribute to the family's alcoholic dynamics. In short, compulsiveness helps enablers to deny the reality of their own and the family's situation.

# WORRIERS

Enablers are *worriers* who are unwilling or unable to see alcoholism or the insidious effects of it in the family. Like the alcoholic they tend to see the drink problem as being all outside of themselves and they see little or no connection between themselves and the problem. Despite this myopic view of their situation, perhaps because of it, they worry a lot.

The worry of many enablers comes in waves. Sometimes they feel inundated by it. At other times free of it. When worried they have to go into action, "do something" for the alcoholic or for another member of the family to assuage the constant sense of guilt with which they live. The guilt can derive from the abuse they inflict on others in the family or for the abuse others inflict upon them. Both worry and guilt seem to keep them on an emotional roller coaster.

Enablers are enablers because of their need to control and dominate the alcoholic or because they are emotionally or economically dependent on the alcoholic. In either case they are unwilling, usually see themselves as unable, to change their lives. In both cases they spend their lives in worry.

The dependent enablers are sometimes physically abused. When that is the case they usually develop an alcoholic-like view of being victimized by life and circumstances. Too often they develop a masochistic outlook and learn to suffer in silence. Occasionally these enabler's develop a martyr complex much as if they are ennobling their suffering by doing so. Happiness of any kind, even a modicum of it, they conclude, is not for this life but in the next only.

What people think is of critical importance to enablers. Indeed, it determines and explains much about their behavior. Typical enabler thinking goes like this:

"What will people think if they find out my wife is alcoholic?"

"If I leave him?"

"If they were to stop in, when she's roaring drunk?"

"If he/she lets the lawn go too long?"

"If she/he gets into an auto accident when she's/he's drunk?"

*This obsessive concern for appearances and propriety is a major reason enablers persevere in their enabling, a major reason they have so many worries.*

## CASE OF THE CAHILL FAMILY

The following story is a true one and is of a family which I saw in counseling for just under five months. The only fictions are their names, the location of their house, and their occupations. Their physical descriptions have been altered, albeit only a little bit. The dynamics and the intra-familial relationship are real. The verbal exchanges of the counseling sessions have been edited and descriptions added only to make the whole account more readable.

Bernard Cahill called me twice for an appointment then left word twice with my answering service that he couldn't make it. He gave no explanation. Several weeks after these cancellations he called again. I took this third call myself. He sounded frantic and wanted an appointment immediately. He became irritated when I told him I was booked for that day and the following one but would see him after hours at 9 p.m. on Wednesday.

He was pacing in the waiting room when I opened the office door at 8:55. Bernard is of average height, black hair cut short. I was to learn that he is in his early forties but the lines on his face make him seem older. He was impeccably dressed in a three piece dark suit, light blue shirt, striped maroon, and white tie. I seldom see a client so formally dressed at such a late hour.

He seemed so tightly wound that I thought it better to dispense with the routine personal questions and made small talk to help abate the usual first session anxieties. As he relaxed back into the lounge chair he seemed to wind down. His voice lost its tension, modulated and he talked in a more relaxed fashion.

*"I heard that you specialize in marital counseling doctor. That's why I need to see you."*

I nodded. *"So what are the problems?"*

He looked at me, looked away, shook his head, *"I don't know what they are. That's the crazy part. I don't know."*

His confusion and bewilderment seemed honest.

*"I called and cancelled twice. For me that's crazy. I'm not like that. An appointment made is a commitment. I never break a commitment. I'm acting just as crazy as she is. I called because we were fighting. She was screaming at me, at the kids, at Nan especially. Then I'd cancel because suddenly it all seemed better."*

*"This last time you didn't cancel."*

He shook his head. *"No. I had to see you. She beat Nan up—bad. She's never done anything like that. We have to see you. Something's very wrong."*

*"But you don't know what."*

*"No, I don't."*

*"Has your wife agreed to see me?"*

*"Yes."*

*"Why didn't she come tonight too?"*

*"Shy. She's very shy. Embarrassed too."*

*"About what?"*

*"About how she's been acting. Feels bad about it."*

*"I see."* (Those were my words. Actually I didn't see I was puzzled and doubted what he was telling me. Was she embarrassed about seeing me because of her behavior at home? Was that the real reason or was there something else? I had the impression that Bernard was not telling me all he could, for some reason was holding back. I would find out.)

I spent the balance of the session getting basic data about the Cahill family. He is 41, his wife Martha, 39. They have two children: a son, Sam 16 and a junior in high school, and a daughter, Nan 14 and in her first year of high school. Bernard is an accountant in a large industrial firm in Springfield. His wife was a secretary, before they were married, but hasn't worked in almost seventeen years.

*"She worked before the kids were born and hasn't since. We figured she should stay home with the kids. We didn't want our kids brought up by a lot of baby sitters. That's the reasons so many kids are in so much trouble today. They never had a mother at home."*

I smiled. *"Mothers belong at home."*

He nodded. *"For sure."*

I made an appointment for him and Martha for the following Monday evening. The Cahill's live on one of the main thoroughfares of our town. It's an unusually wide street shaded with maples and elms. It's the street I drive through to and from work. I had noticed the house, more particularly the grounds before I knew he lived there. It was a place most people would notice. It wasn't the house, an ordinary colonial. It was the landscaping.

Driving by the next morning I looked closely. Yes, positively flawless. The lawn was a vivid green and manicured. The shrubs appeared to be shaped by a razor. The several small trees were pruned to perfection, not a twig was out of place. I grinned. It all fit with Bernard's impeccable three piece suit.

### Sessions 1 Through 4

### All About The Unspoken Problem

I ushered them in promptly at seven on the following Monday night. Bernard, in a camel hair blazer and sharply creased navy blue pants, still looked like he had just stepped out of a Brooks Brothers emporium. He seemed more relaxed than last time as he had a broad smile on his face. Martha seemed worried or scared or both. I couldn't tell. Her thin mouth was set tightly. Her brown eyes were narrowed. She looked down when we said hello and held out a wet, limp hand. Martha gave me the distinct impression that she wished she were anywhere but in my office. I remembered Bernard's assessment that she was shy. She certainly seemed so on initial contact.

Martha's general appearance can best be described as non-descript, about five feet four, light brown hair, and I would estimate 150 pounds. Martha's overweight.

They sat on the two seat couch. Bernard draped his arm casually between the back of the couch and her shoulders. He began brightly, *"Well here we are."*

I looked at Martha, *"My impression is you're not too happy to be here."*

*"But she is!"* Bernard said in the same bright tone.

*"Are you?"* I asked.

She glanced away and smiled the little wan smile with which I was to become so familiar in the next months. *"Yes, I am."* Her tone was something less than positive.

I looked at Bernard, spoke gently. *"A basic rule in couple or marital counseling is that we never talk for each other, only to each other."*

Bernard nodded.

*"Martha, Bernard tells me that there are a lot of problems at home. That lately you've been acting erratically—-Do you want to talk about it?"*

Martha gave a loud sigh. *"If I've been acting awful. It's not all my fault."*

*"I'm sure."*

*"Are you saying it's mine?"* Bernard's look and tone were sharp.

Martha didn't answer, just made her little smile.

*"We're not interested in finding fault. We just want to understand what's going on and why it is."* I said.

Bernard nodded. *"That's all we want."*

*"Martha, how would you describe how you feel right now,"* I asked slowly, softly.

She looked at me directly for the first time. *"Very alone."* She said in a sad but surprisingly firm voice.

Bernard gave a loud sigh. *"I know we're all different but alone? Alone? How can you feel alone? You've got two kids who love you and me."* Bernard looked at me flabbergasted. *"See, that's what I meant when I said we've got problems but not knowing what they are."*

*"Bernie, you tell me every day that our problems are my problems."*

I had suspected that. *"What do you tell her Bernard."*

Bernard looked at her nonplused, back at me embarrassedly. *"I tell her that maybe she should do more at home."*

The withering look Martha shot him jibed with her sneering tone. *"Bernie, if nothing else, you really know how to color the truth to convince everybody, yourself included, that you're being honest."*

*"I'm not lying,"* he said.

*"No,"* she said softly, *"you're not, but why don't you tell him how you criticize every blessed thing I do, my cooking, even how I dust."* She turned to me. *"You want to hear something? Once I spent the day scrubbing floors, vacuuming, dusting, cleaning the house to perfection, absolute perfection. You know what he said? Do you want to know what*

*his comment was after inspecting the house? The philodendrum can stand dusting, Martie. That's what he said! He couldn't find anything else. So he found a plant needed dusting. A goddamned plant,"* she screamed. *"That's what I've been living with."*

*Bernard looked mortified, gave his own wan little smile. He took his arm back from behind her, moved away a little from her. "All I meant by that was a plant just will not thrive if the leaves have dust on them. Plants are one of my hobbies,"* he explained looking at me.

*"Bernie,"* she said drily, *"you're the only person I know who thinks plants should be dusted."* She looked at me. *"Sam has to dust the plants once a week."*

*"They're my hobby."* he repeated.

*"Well they're not Sam's, nor mine either,"* she screamed. *"Why don't you dust them?"*

*"Why, why? Because I do everything now that's why."*

Martha sighed. *"Bernie you're a driven man about all the important things in life like philodrendra."*

*"Well, we're all different,"* he grinned.

Martha's response was another withering look. *"We're all different. We're all different. You're always saying that lately. And you don't believe it one tiny bit!"*

*"But I do!"*

*"Oh, that's shit and you know it. Bernie,"* she said through clench-ed teeth. *"What you really think is that anybody who's different from you is weird. Like Sam says, 'In your opinion to be different is to be weird.' For once in your life admit what's true."*

*"That's not true,"* he said hotly.

Martha shrugged, *"Ah, what's the use?"*

I spoke, *"Quite obviously you're very upset with Bernard. You're major irritation seems to come from the fact that he's uh—very particular about how things are done and—"*

*"Not that,"* Martha corrected.

*"What then?"*

*"He puts me down for what I am and how I am and he's always doing it in front of the kids."* Right then Martha started to cry.

Bernie gave her a disgusted look, shrugged and said to me. *"That's what she does whenever things get a little tense."*

I looked at him. His lack of sensitivity needed a jolt and badly. *"Bernard,"* I said slowly. *"The impression you give me is that you feel that the problems in your marriage are all Martha's."*

He looked at me surprised then responded in a tone properly apologetic. *"No, no. I don't feel that way at all. Martha's problems are hers but they're mine too."*

*"Mine first though, eh?"* Martha said with her little smile.

Bernard looked exasperated. *"You're saying that. You know I didn't mean that."*

*"The basic problem,"* said Martha cocking her head toward her husband, *"is that he's a steamroller."*

Bernard's flush indicated he was both embarrassed and angry. His response communicated both feelings. *"My God Martha, what a thing to say."*

She had to feel the vitriolic look he was giving her. I chuckled, hoping to lighten the sudden tension. *"You want to explain what you mean? And, uh—address Bernard."*

Martha shrugged, looked down. *"Bernie, you want to do everything, run everything and you know it."*

Bernard's response crackled with fury. *"If if I do, it's because I have to. You don't do anything."*

Martha made her little smile. *"He calls me mummified Martha."*

*"Well damnit, you are."*

Bernard looked at me. *"She never moves. She's in a perpetual state of immobility. She sits in her chair in the living room and reads. Period. I have to do everything. I even have to do the ironing now. She'll let it pile up for weeks. We've all learned that our shirts, socks, underwear, you name it, are in the dryer or the clothes basket. They're never in our drawers, where they're supposed to be. If we complain she tells me and the kids that we don't have enough clothes. That we need to buy more. My son cleans the house, Nan makes the beds, gets supper, and, would you believe I, me, I do the ironing. She does nothing. It's a disgrace."*

Martha looked at him, responded as if he hadn't said a word. *"Mummified Martha,"* she repeated. *"You call me that in front of the kids."*

*"What really hurts is that he doesn't show you any respect in front of the kids."*

*"He puts me down all the time, anywhere and everywhere."*

*"I don't,"* he roared. *"I don't put you down in front of other people. I never do!"*

*"I've got no respect at home,"* Martha insisted. *"Not from you and not from Nan either."*

*"If you don't, it's your own fault and you know it."*

Their hostility was reflected not only in the words but in the tones and especially in their glares and in the fact that they had both edged to the opposite ends of the couch.

> **Counselor's Comments:** By now we were into our third meeting. Martha's shyness at the initial meeting had pretty much evaporated. What I had learned in the process of that evaporation was that her little wan smile like her shyness were poor and very thin veneers for a resistant and very angry woman.
>
> What I had learned too, was that Bernard's concern for appearances was genuine and was not just for strangers. It was very much for family too. It was reflected in his abiding concern and demands about the doing and completion of household chores—beds made, house cleaned, ironing done, supper ready.

Martha responded with indifference, an indifference born of anger and one which drove Bernard to distraction. Martha, of course, knew that and persevered in her indifference. Yes, Martha was a very angry woman. Bernard's intrusive, demeaning and controlling ways explained much of the why of that anger but not all of it. I knew, more accurately felt, that much should have been said by now which had not been said.

Suddenly Bernard's glaring look softened. He sighed loudly, looked at his wife kindly and whispered out, *"Why don't you just tell him, Martie?"*

*"What should I tell him?"*

The innocent tone was transparently feigned and just didn't jibe with her remarkable candor to that point.

Bernard shook his head, a very pained look on his face.

*"Bernie thinks I have a drinking problem."*

I was not surprised. All the enabling and alcoholic symptoms were by now transparent to me. I looked at Bernard. *"Why didn't you tell me the first time you saw me?"*

Bernard answered slowly. *"It's Martie's problem. All the books, all the pamphlets, say she's the one who should talk about it, not me."*

*"When are you going to be honest about yourself, about us?"*

*"Look who's talking about honest! You won't even admit you've got the problem."*

*"I'm not sure I do."*

*"Then why do you hide your drinks?"*

*"Because you make me feel guilty. That's why."*

*"Rot!"*

*"Not rot,"* she screamed. *"True."*

I nodded. *"My impression is you're both telling the truth as you see it. But Martha if you have an alcohol problem here we're not going to resolve any problems in this marriage until you stop drinking and Bernard starts changing some of his ways."*

*"I don't know that I have an alcohol problem."*

*"You do,"* cried Bernard.

*"How do I know?"* she asked me. I never cease to marvel at the honesty and innocence with which that question is always asked.

*"Is it affecting your life with Bernard and your children?"*

*"It's not just the drink that's doing it. It's, it's everything.*

*"Does alcohol make anything better?"*

*"Sometimes it does."*

Bernard spoke quietly. *"Maybe for you but not for the rest of us. You're only decent at home when you're on your first drink. After that you're very mad or very sad, darling. There doesn't seem to be any in between."*

It was the first time Bernard had used any term of endearment. He was trying hard to communicate.

Martha turned to me. *"What about him? You said he's got to change some of his ways. He's part of this too, isn't he?"*

I nodded. *"If you have a problem with drink, my impression is that you, Bernard, helped it along."*

This time Martha put on a broad grin. *"Hallelujah"* she cried. *"Somebody finally said it."*

*"How could I have helped it along?"* There was no anger in Bernard's tone, no surprise even, just curiousity.

*"How? How?"* Martha cried. *"By trying to take over everything. Like I said you steamroller over me and Sam too. And Nan has become just like you."*

*"If I do that, it's because I love you. I, I worry about you and the kids,"* he said lamely, retreating into a whisper.

*"These are some of the things we need to talk about, Bernard. How you express your love and like I said, you, Martha have to decide if you have a problem and if you do, you have to determine if it's affecting Bernard and the children."*

End of the first four sessions.


## Session 5

In Session 5 Martha admitted to her addiction, revealed that she had already attended several A.A. meetings. Her best judgement was that her drinking had been out of control for just over six months. Her most memorable line in this regard was *"It became bad right after he started calling me mummified in front of the kids."*

At the same session a subdued Bernard verbalized several times that he wanted to change his ways *"so that we can all get on better as a family."*

What had become transparent during these first five sessions was that Bernard and Martha's problems extended to and involved their children. It was for that reason that my next four appointments were made with all four Cahills together.


## Sessions 6 Through 8

### Relationships

The Cahills arrived together and on time for the sixth session. Nancy and Sam, I observed look a little bit like both parents. Nancy is her mother's height but the similarity with her ends there. She inherited her father's black hair and like him wears it close cropped. She also has his pinched, anxious look. Her brother, Sam, wears his black hair in a modified punk style (straight up but only in front). He's round faced and like his mother is overweight. Bernard and Martha took their usual seats on the couch. Nan took a seat next to Bernard's side of the couch. Sam sat on my right facing his parents.

I opened up the session with, *"I've been seeing your mother and father now for over a month. We think we have the problems pretty well defined."*

*"So why did you want Sam and me to be here tonight?"* asked Nancy. *"We don't have anything to do with her drinking."* She spoke in a bored, irritated tone.

*"But you're affected by it."* I said quickly.

She nodded. *"You're right, and I've got the bruises to show for it."* Then she added determinedly *"But I'm not going to be affected anymore, for sure."*

*"That's silly, Nan,"* said Bernard. *"We're all in the same family. We live in the same house."*

*"Maybe. But daddy, we're not all alcoholic."*

I shook my head. *"When you live with an alcoholic you can react to the alcohol in ways that make you act and react like an alcoholic, even if you're not drinking."*

Nan looked at me impatiently, *"What's that mean?"*

I leaned toward her, spoke gently but earnestly. *"What you just said there so emphatically, that you weren't going to be affected by your mother's drinking shows that you already were and that you've pretty much made up your mind that you're going to shut her out of your life."*

Nancy shrugged. I turned to Martha. *"How's that make you feel?"*

Martha sighed. *"I knew all this. It's why I told you way back that I feel alone."* Martha looked at Nancy. *"You're your father's daughter."*

Nancy gave a little false laugh. *"Well I hope so, mother."* Her laugh vanished. *"Otherwise I'd be illegitimate and a bitch. A bitch like you."*

Bernard cried out. *"Nancy how can you talk to your mother like that?"*

Martha shrugged, spoke wearily. *"She can, she does, and you know it."*

*"No, I don't know it,"* he replied heatedly. *"At least I never heard her call you a bitch before."*

Martha nodded. *"She has before. The last time she did I beat her. That's why I did. I was reduced to that to get respect. She's—"* Martha turned toward her daughter. *"You never show me any respect."*

*"Well, you never show me anything. No love, or caring, or concern. Until you beat on me you never even showed me any anger. I'll never forgive you for that beating mother. Never!"*

Nancy said all that in steel-like tones but those tones did not jibe with the expression in her eyes. She looked like she wanted to cry. For a split second I thought she might.

*"I was drunk when I did that,"* Martha said slowly. *"I don't know if that's an excuse. A.A. says it isn't. I'm just starting to realize now what I did, what happened. I went a little crazy. Maybe it was because of that defiant, arrogant look you put on. Maybe it was because you called me a bitch, I just don't know—"* She trailed off.

*"I still didn't deserve to be beaten,"* said Nancy.

*"No one does,"* said Martha in a small voice.

Nancy stood up and cried out, *"Why do you say it like that. 'No one does!' Why don't you say, no you didn't deserve it Nancy."*

Nancy didn't wait for a reply. *"I know why. It's what drives me nuts about you. You never even can admit you did something wrong especially to me."*

*"Poor, poor abused Nan."* Sam spoke his first words.

We all looked at him.

*"I am abused!"* Nan cried.

*"Bullshit. You deserved it,"* he said loconically. *"She should've done it five years ago. Ma's right. You never show her respect."*

*"Of course you'd say that you always take her part."* glared Nan.

*"I wish we'd all stop siding against one another,"* said Bernard in a loud plaintive voice.

Martha chuckled. *"Funny how when Nan sides with you against me you never notice. When Sam sides with me you do."*

*"What's that supposed to mean?"*

*"Just that. You see what you want too."*

Bernard looked exasperated. *"All I want is peace and harmony,"* he cried. *"If I've done what you say, I was wrong. All right? I don't want any of us taking sides or ganging up on each other anymore."*

Bernard paused a moment looked at me. *"Martha's right. Nan sides with me. Sam with her. Why do we do that?"*

*"Has to do with how you all see each other, especially how you see Sam and Nan,"* I answered.

*"I don't know how I see them, as you put it, but I treat them exactly alike."*

Sam cupped his hands megaphone-like around his mouth, *"More bullshit."*

Bernard's eyes widened. *"It is not bullshit. That's true!"*

Sam leaned back, his eyes narrowed, his words came out soft, gentle. *"Dad, no offense but the truth is you see Nan as a winner and me as a loser."*

*"Not a loser,"* his father roared.

*"O.K. maybe loser's too strong. Let's just say not as swift or as uh, uh competent."*

Bernard didn't answer.

Martha turned to me. *"As you can see, we're a family divided."*

*"Yes, divided into two hostile camps and each person has an ally. And what I've learned is that you all have contributed to the hostile*

*camp. You Martha, by your withdrawal and lack of involvement in the family and especially with Nancy whom I suspect wants to be closer to you. A while ago she looked like she wanted to cry because she doesn't feel or know how to get closer to you. Bernard, you've contributed to the division by using demeaning terms toward Martha which Nancy has picked up on. The way you compare Sam to Nancy puts Sam down. The end result of that is that Sam, you don't want to identify with your father but with your mother because you see her and yourself too, as the under-dogs, as the non-achievers in a family where you Bernard have made achievement a basic reason if not the basic reason for living. You Nancy have identified more with your father than your mother and I suspect, not sure yet, you're not too comfortable with that."*

*"So what's all that mean,"* asked Bernard a little bewilderedly.

Even as he asked the question I realized that my long summary and intepretation had been very clinical, interesting to a practicing psychotherapist but not terribly meaningful or practical to a client.

I chuckled. *"What it all means is that you are all losing by maintaining an allied and hostile camp setting. Martha, you talked about feeling alone. The truth is that you all feel alone."* I looked at each in turn and they all nodded.

### Counselor's Comments

We spent the rest of this eighth session discussing how important it was to dissolve the alliances and how important it was to get closer, each to the other three. My impression from the start had been that Bernard's perception of his family and of his own self would be the key areas to explore. I was confident that the Cahill family problems stemmed in considerable measure from his enabler-like personality. His overprotective, compulsive, and worrying ways had done much to facilitate Martha's alcoholism and generally to create emotional havoc in the family. These explorations I felt would be better done with him and Martha alone. Such discussions I had learned, usually get into concerns private to the parents. For this reason the next several sessions were with Bernard and Martha only.

## Sessions 9 Through 11

## Happy Endings

I began the ninth session with the question, *"Bernard what are the first words which come to mind which really describe you."*

Bernard answered in less than an eyewink. *"Devoted to my family, responsible, hardworking, and caring."* He nodded. *"That's how I would describe me."*

Martha looked amused. She also looked more relaxed than I'd ever seen her. *"How would you describe Bernard?"*

She closed her eyes, spoke slowly. *"Domineering, perfectionist, driven, lives with a lot of useless anxiety."*

I nodded. *"Now, as I see it a lot of the Cahill family problems lie in the difference just expressed. If you can both come closer to what's really true, the problems should dissipate."*

*"Let's do that for Martha,"* Bernard said spiritedly.

I nodded toward her. Again she closed her eyes. *"Addictive, low-opinion of me, dependent and I'm anxious just like Bernie."*

*"You, Bernie,"* I said.

*"I would have said addictive too, for obvious reasons and slow-moving and low self-esteem but I never would have pegged you as being very anxious about very much, Martha."*

*"Your perceptions of Martha are pretty comparable. Now that Martha admits to her problem and maintains her sobriety there won't be much conflict or problems from your mutual perceptions of her."*

*"I'm the problem, eh?"*

*"No, not you but like I said the difference in views you both have of her."*

"So what do we do?" Bernard asked.

"How much can you accept of what she said about you?"

He nodded. "It's true. I am a perfectionist. But what's so bad about that?"

I looked at Martha.

"Not too much really," she said, "except when you expect us to be the same way." She looked at me. "I've started cooking again, because I know I should and he's begun hovering again. Yesterday I was making a stew and you were hovering over me like I'd never done it before. So what if it didn't come out perfect?"

"True," he said sheepishly, "I hover. I promise to stay out of the kitchen."

Martha looked at him grimly. "Not just the kitchen Bernie, out of our lives."

"What? What are you saying?"

"Bernie you have to give me and the kids some space."

"But Martha," he said in dead earnest, "I'm a husband, a father. Most people would still call me the head of the family. I've got a right to—"

"Recommend and suggest. Period. You have no right to run our lives. We're not babies, not me nor the kids either. I have to run mine and the kids have to run theirs. I can't speak for the kids but you were taking over my soul. And I let you. That's my fault. Not going to happen again. I'm resolved about that."

There was a pause as we all digested her resolution.

She continued. "You know what I don't understand, Bernie?"

"What?"

"Why you've always given Nan so much space and why you've been so terrible with Sam."

He nodded. *"I don't know why but I've wondered about it too. Strange, I've always expected more from Sam and Nan has always delivered more. I'm not sure why I expected more. Maybe because fathers expect more from their sons. She's turned out more competent than—"*

*"That's what Sam said you'd say. And that's what you've got to stop,"* she cried. *"You've got to stop comparing them."* She looked at me. *"Right?"*

I nodded emphatically, *"Right!"*

There was a long pause.

*"You know Bernie you really almost destroyed me, and my shame was that I almost let it happen."* She turned to me, *"There's a lot we haven't told you."*

I figured that.

*"Right after I got pregnant I stopped working. I shouldn't but I did because I was in quotes 'a good, submissive wife.' What I was really was was stupid. I never should have quit. Anyway I did. A year ago Bernie broke the news that pretty soon I had to go back to work to help pay college tuitions. Well that made me nervous. Very nervous and angry too. After sixteen years, suddenly I had to become a secretary again. It terrified me. Believe it or not that's what got me started on drinking."*

*"I believe,"* I said nodding. *"Are you going back to work?"*

*"Yes. For me as much as for the tuitions. I used to be a very good secretary and I'm just beginning to realize that I can be again."*

*"She's taking a refresher course at the community college,"* Bernie said.

*"Good!"*

## Session 12

I had only one more session with the Cahills and this one included Nancy and Sam. The session was interesting as it was characterized by virtually no hostility and more importantly, the Sam—Martha and the Bernard—Nancy alliances never surfaced once. On several occasions however, on the subject of curfews and their enforcement, Bernard and Martha teamed up against each teen-ager.

**Later**

Martha is working as a secretary now and although she attends A.A. but rarely she is maintaining her sobriety. It's now been four years.

All the evidence is that Bernard has learned to curb his more destructive enabler dispositions. However, I couldn't help smiling this morning as I drove by his house. His lawn is still the most impeccably maintained of any in town.

**Counselor's Notes**

What this case shows is that a family can indeed recover from its alcoholic ways if the spouses are genuinely motivated to do so. That Bernard's concern was genuine, was reflected in that he not only set out to learn about the dynamics of alcoholism by reading about it but he came for help.

Martha's motivation (more accurately, determination) to recover began with the admission to her addiction, and with the admission that she submitted and even rewarded Bernard's enabling ways.

Finally, the Cahill story ended happily because both enablers and alcoholic *acted* upon their motivation. The point. *Both enabler and alcoholic have to change their destructive ways if a family is going to move toward health.*

## CASE OF ONE SPOUSE, NOT BOTH, MOVING TOWARD HEALTH

The alcoholic story does not end so happily when only one of the spouses moves toward health. The following story, related by a 54 year old woman, shows that and more.

*How did I get to this day? I keep asking myself as I walk across State Street with my attorney. We're walking to ask the court to end my 28 year marriage. I am filled with a whole mixture of feelings—anxiety in facing the unknown, sadness in feeling I have somehow failed in a commitment, and loneliness realizing that I no longer will be looked at by the world as part of that respectable group called "married" but rather viewed as a divorcee. Yes, I also feel some shame for what I'm doing.*

*What made me end the charade? My memory plays back over the 28 years. I realize that I can not identify any happy times with my husband. All the little happinesses seem centered around my daughter. I am surprised by this but comforted too. It makes me feel that what I am doing is right.*

*My first memory of something not quite right is approximately 25 years ago when I was cleaning the unfinished 2nd floor of our cape style home. I found approximately 20 or more empty liquor bottles plus empty beer cans. I was completely dumbfounded. I had no idea what this all meant. I had been brought up in an Irish Catholic family where liquor was not allowed. It was an unknown and a mystery to me. Drinking was something that in the movies was always funny and never serious. The only movie I saw where drinking was viewed as a problem was one with Ray Milland called "Lost Weekend". But that was "just a movie." Situations like that didn't happen in my life.*

*I felt that my husband had deceived me, was lying to me and I didn't understand why he would do such a thing. I just didn't think of a drinking problem. I certainly was naive. I wanted so desperately to trust him and believe in him that I didn't let myself even think that there could be anything else to it.*

*As time went on however, Bill's drinking became more and more evident and more destructive. I stopped having people in. We really stopped socializing as a couple, I was careful who I saw and where. Most of my social life was outside the home, i.e., going to plays or concerts with friends. He was always very glad to have me go out. When I would try to entice him to accompany me he would suggest that I "find somebody to go with" and would cheerfully volunteer to watch our daughter so I wouldn't have to worry about looking for a sitter. I realize now that he did this because he couldn't drink while watching a play or a concert.*

The story of our life together is the story of a woman who loved not wisely and who enabled too well. It was a life of excuses—all made by me for gatherings missed, or his erratic behavior with my family. It was a life of lies too; to my friends about gifts not given to me, about wedding anniversaries not celebrated, about my birthday not remembered. And then there was Christmas. The Eve spent alone, the day trying to keep some semblance of happiness in the family—basically for my daughter's sake.

Eventually I went to work full time, primarily to save for college tuition for Cathy. I was extremely fortunate in that the company I went to work for had a tuition refund program. I enrolled in a local college and was able to complete both a bachelor's degree in business and a master's degree. I realize now that while this helped my career it also afforded me a way not to look at the situation I was living in. The pursuit of my studies became a vehicle for me to deny and not to confront and face the emptiness of my life.

My employer also had an Employees Assistance Program. In that program was a substance abuse counselor and a psychologist. I started talking to the counselor, casually, at lunch asking questions around alcoholism. I realized that I had a tremendous amount to learn. Eventually I started seeing the psychologist and it was through him that I was able to understand the role I had played. I was a classic enabler. I did all kinds of things that I thought would keep my husband busy and not drinking, i.e., bought a camper because I believed that camping is a family style vacation. The first time we went away with the camper, the cases of beer took up so much of the trunk space that all the tools needed had to be put on the back seat. I realize that only now as I write this. I also bought a home computer. I thought this would really keep him busy and get him interested in something besides watching T.V. I thought that if he was busy he wouldn't have time to drink. I also felt if I took more responsibility it would lessen the stress on him and then maybe he wouldn't feel the need for drinking. You know what I learned? Nothing works! The alcoholic continues to make you feel guilty for his drinking and until you can get through that, your hooked into it.

Via marriage I became manipulated by alcohol even though I was not the alcoholic. I was allowing liquor to design the structure of my life. Alcohol became the center around which decisions were made, when my husband and I would "go out", i.e., what time of day, who we would be seeing. It also became a "family member." How? By our method of communicating or rather, not communicating. By the mundane subjects we allowed ourselves to discuss the weather, the lawn and believe it or not even the color of homes on the street where we lived! We never once confronted the "intruder" who was basically destroying the relationship.

Does it make sense to place blame and responsibility on an inaminate object such as alcohol? Or should the person who uses it really carry the burden of guilt? I still ask myself these questions. But really what difference does it make? What I have learned is that the alcoholic becomes the liquid and inebriates the rest of the family.

I realize finally that change doesn't happen because you want it to. The other person must recognize the problem and want to change. I divorced him. I realize now that the divorce actually occurred a long, long time ago. It occurred when alcohol became Bill's all consuming mistress. The first thing I noticed after he moved out was that the quality of my life had improved. I had always taken on responsibility for the maintenance of the home so I really did not have any additional tasks to perform. It became a pleasure to unlock the door, walk into the house, and feel the peace within. This was a new feeling for me, something I hadn't experienced during my whole marriage. I lost my feeling of guilt. Guilt is everywhere when dealing with an alcoholic. I found that to effect change, to place a value on myself, to start to address my own needs I had to rid myself of the guilt. I've done so.

When I was divorced, my daughter was 25 years old. I was told by well meaning friends that the divorce would not affect her. In some ways they were right, but what I had not realized was that the dynamics of the life she grew up in had affected her tremendously. Cathy is pretty, bright but has a weight problem. Still she has always managed to achieve goals that she set for herself. She had graduated from college with a B.S. in Biology and then decided to go into nursing. During the divorce process she was a candidate for a Bachelor's Degree in Nursing. After graduation she came home and started to look for a job in Boston. She didn't seem to be having any luck. I would come home from work and find her sitting in her father's chair, with a tall glass of water, watching T.V., a pile of candy wrappers in the ashtray. When I asked her about applications, potential interviews, and so forth, she would tell me that no one was hiring, she called here, she called there, or she didn't feel well, "think I am coming down with a cold", she'd say in a depressed little voice.

*I felt I was living a replay of my life with Bill. The only thing different was that the wrappers were in plain sight. He always hid his drinks behind the chair. He'd used the same excuses when things didn't turn out as he felt they should. Everything seemed to happen to him rather than he controlling what happened. Her behavior was mirroring his.*

*I was really upset. I had lived alone for a couple of months and in this period of aloneness had come to see and understand how I had let myself be cast into the role of enabler. I could see myself being drawn into that role again. I didn't want it! The whole family loses when one member enables. I decided to confront her. I laid out my expectations. To her credit and my relief she responded positively. She went out, interviewed and found an excellent job. She also found her own apartment. I'm convinced she did both because I put the responsibility back where it belonged—on her shoulders.*

*I feel alone today but not lonely, different than I felt when I was married. I always felt lonely then. I also, strange as it may seem, feel more responsible for myself even though in reality I have always been. It is as though my aloneness is magnified by living alone. I try to watch myself when I feel that "ole enabler" creeping up on me because it really doesn't help me but more importantly, it doesn't help the other person either.*

*The end of any relationship is sad and I live with a deep sense of loss. I think of what might have been and what will never be. Then every once in a while I think of a marriage wasted.*

*Nevertheless, my hope for a better life remains. Even though I'm uncertain where I'm headed what I know is that I've left the craziness behind me. I'm in transition. That fact makes me feel proud for it means I did what most people are too afraid to do—change. It was this idea that Emerson was explaining when he wrote "Not in his goals but in his transitions is a person great."*

**Notation**

What we learn from this story is that sometimes *the pain, guilt, embarrassment, and humiliation of living with an alcoholic can become so great that one may seek an alternative life style* as in divorce.

A prime inhibitor to divorce for this woman, as for many, was guilt. Her realization that her husband via his alcohol had divorced the family a long time ago helped much to assuage that guilt.

Another common inhibitor to divorce is fear of not being able to cope alone with life. This woman's sudden realization that her husband would not change helped her overcome that fear. This fresh perspective combined with her newly found refusal to continue playing the role of enabler made her realize that there was simply no other role for her to play in the tragedy which was her marriage. Ergo, she did as many have done and will do, she divorced.

# Chapter 3

# COMMUNICATION

Communication can occur on three levels: the verbal, the emotional, and the physiological. The most honest, most effective communications occur when our words jibe with our feelings and are reflected on our faces and in our body stance. When the three levels fit together in the message we are delivering we feel good and the message gets through loudly and clearly. When the word content does not go with our emotional tone and/or facial expression then the message may well get garbled.

Healthy families are those where each member feels free and is open to communication. In families such as these communication is so good that each member's needs, feelings, and concerns don't have to be expressed verbally. Indeed, in such families communication is so exquisite and other oriented that messages are anticipated and accurately, so well so that members know and identify with each other.

*In alcoholic families communication is at best restrained, generally bewildering, often non-existent.* Members do not feel free to express themselves and/or are closed to accepting communications with one another. This lack of communication is what differentiates the alcoholic family from the healthy family. Often this lack facilitates the alcoholism. Always it maintains it.

A major reason that communication is poor in the alcoholic family is that the relationship between spouses is unequal. An unequal relationship is one where the dominant spouse communicates by blaming and condemning. The other, in turn, feeds into the domineering spouse's system of communication by reacting in a passive and/or submissive way. In an unequal relationship like this both parties come to feel demeaned. The submissive one for obvious reasons; the dominant one because he/she loses respect because of the other's passivity and dependency. Communication ceases.

These dynamics prevail in the alcoholic family even if neither of the spouses is alcoholic. *The point is that a family can communicate as an alcoholic family even if no one in the family ingests alcohol.* In such cases either or both of the spouses usually have a history of alcoholism in their families of origin and/or extended families. In either or both settings they learned alcoholic methods of communication. Via these methods the parent(s) can structure family interaction and relationships so children learn to communicate in an alcoholic way or even worse, to become alcoholic.

The principal methods of communication in the alcoholic family are

    1. double messages,
    2. compartmentalization,
    3. arbitrariness,
    4. elusiveness,
    5. intellectualization, and
    6. indifference.

The family might not use all of these modes but only some of them. Or indeed may obsess on only one.

# DOUBLE MESSAGES

*Double messages* are those where the words spoken do not jibe with the emotional tones on which they ride or on the behavior displayed. The enabler who nags his/her alcoholic spouse about drinking is delivering a double message when he/she pours the spouse another drink. The alcoholic man who brings chocolates and flowers home to his wife then after several drinks physically abuses her is doing the same. The wife who screams "No I'm not angry," at her inebriated husband when he spills Burgandy wine on the new linen tablecloth is also delivering a double message. We are all familiar with double messages. They can and do occur on occasion even in healthy families. In alcoholic families they are a principal mode of communication.

Not uncommonly, alcoholic parents were themselves steeped and reared in homes where double messages were, if not the prime mode of familial interaction, then at least a common one. These modes they pass on to their children.

Children are the ones who are most vulnerable to double messages. They find double messages confusing and bewildering. How do they respond to a slurred, tight lipped message such as this, "Yes children, you can play with the ball. Just be sure to play quietly. Mother's not feeling well. She has that awful migraine again." The words themselves are confusing. Yes they can play. But how can they play *quietly* with a ball? The veiled threat is communicated that, if any noise at all exists, there will be hell to pay. Besides all that, the tone says don't play. Such a message leaves children in a dilemna. If they play, they play with the anxiety of incurring mother's drunken wrath—or they don't play at all. The latter, which they choose often, results in insufferable boredom. This is why boredom is a common fate of children in alcoholic families.

Perhaps the most devastating effect upon children reared in a double message system is that they never learn to value the truth because they never know what the truth is. Not only do they not know what the messages they get mean but just as importantly they never learn to *feel* about the messages they get. *People reared in a system of double messages frequently become alienated from their own feelings.* They don't know how they feel because they don't know what's true. Indeed truth, to them, especially in communication, becomes an irrelevancy, unimportant. *This is precisely why the children of alcoholics frequently lie when they could just as easily tell the truth.* What they learn as children is that truth is not important or again, lying doesn't really matter.

# COMPARTMENTALIZATION

When people compartmentalize in the family they communicate according to how they perceive their role or the relationship they seek to have with another member. The words, tones, and behaviors they use vary according to role and relationship. The variance and inconsistencies can be considerable. Thus, a man may function as a domineering despot with his wife and as a soft-spoken, malleable Casper Milquetoast with his daughter and revert to the despotic role with his son. Similarly, a woman in her role of wife can play Mrs. Doormat for her husband, and as a mother be coldly indifferent toward her daughter but warmly indulgent toward her son.

Compartmentalization occurs in many families. In reasonably healthy families it is usually latent but fairly well controlled and even discussed and joked about, i.e., terrible tempered daddy treats his daughter like a little princess.

In alcoholic families compartmentalizations are blatant and uncontrolled and like most actualities they are denied. *Among the most harmful effects are that compartmentalizations which occur in alcoholic families engender hostility and create alliances which undermine any loyalty or love which the members might feel.* Thus, the abused, submissive but enabling wife may play on the sympathy of one or more of the children for her plight. In doing so she may be structuring a permanent estrangement between children and their father. The children involved in such unhappy alliances with mother usually lose respect for her as they come to realize that she fed into the neurotic parental alliance. As adults these people usually live out their lives with much anger toward both parents for the emotional havoc and deprivation they were forced to experience in childhood. An even more unfortunate effect for these people is that as children they had no role models from whom they could learn how to relate to the oppostive sex. For example, what can the daughter of a submissive, maternal enabler learn about relating to a man? She can learn that in the context of family life women are supposed to be submissive and that men are dominant and in control. Such learnings usually lead to fear or at least, an untrusting attitude toward men. In any case, in such a situation a girl can learn nothing which is enhancing for her heterosexual life as a woman.

What do boys reared in comparable situations learn about relating to women? If they become especially sympathetic to their mother, they learn to hate their fathers. (This is probably a major reason why so many male children of alcoholics come to have problems with their own sense of self-worth). Frequently they come to feel that women are legitimate objects of scorn, if not abuse.

Girls and boys learn little or nothing positive about how to relate to each other. As a result, they are impoverished. The especial tragedy for both boys and girls is that neither acquires any effective learning in how to relate in a personally rewarding or in an enhancing way to the opposite sex.

## ARBITRARINESS

Arbitrariness is the method of communication of dictators. These people can be alcoholics or they can be enablers. Those who communicate in this manner can not brook questions or even discussion about a decision they made or a point of view they've taken.

Rigidity of position on whatever topic is the most salient characteristic of people who use this communicative method. They *know* that what they believe is right. If they have doubts, they do not show them, nor admit them even to themselves. Their position, points of view, and values seem to be carved in granite.

People who assume arbitrariness as a method close any doors to communication. If family members do not or can not see their point of view, there is nothing to talk about. In the non-alcoholic family arbitrary people invariably engender hostility, start fights, and create distance between and among members. In the alcoholic family all of these unfortunate effects, if anything, are made more acute.

*Arbitrariness is a favorite mode for alcoholics and enablers too.* As a communicative mode it is founded on the denial defense and its prime support is projection. Arbitrary people are simply not prone to look into themselves. Their perceptual stance is "There's nothing wrong inside with me all the wrong is outside with others." Such people can not afford to look in. If they did, they might find themselves wanting and thereby put themselves under conflict, stress to change. Change for the arbitrary person is almost never a viable alternative. This is a reason why alcoholism in an arbitrary person is so very difficult to treat.

Arbitrary people generally tend to have a combative attitude. With arbitary alcoholics this attitude degenerates into heated arguments if not actual fighting. This is especially true in the initital stages of the arbitrary alcoholic's disease and when under the influence. The old John L. Sullivan challenge bawled out in the barroom after several drinks, "I can lick anybody in the house!" pretty well describes the incipient alcoholic's interpersonal stance. If nothing else, lines like these reflect the arbitrary alcoholic's basic hostility, a hostility born of a perception that the world is a kind of battle ground filled with adversaries.

This hostility never leaves arbitrary alcoholics even if they stop drinking. For these alcoholics the hostility goes underground and fuels much good missionary-like work in Alcoholics Anonymous or other socially productive organizations. For those who continue drinking the hostility is complemented by a kind of self-protective withdrawal from social situations and events and brought into the family context where it erupts on the least provocation.

*Arbitrariness in enablers provides an excellent rationalization for alcoholics to continue drinking.* This is especially true of submissive, withdrawn alcoholics. They convince themselves that no way exists with which to cope with the rigidity and unreasonableness, thus they surrender their egos and drink.

The arbitrariness in the alcoholic family is not the arbitrariness found in a non-alcoholic family where the dominant individual might be characterized as a benevolent despot. Alcohol extinguishes benevolence. In the alcoholic family arbitrariness creates a climate where hostility lies on a hair trigger—a rant, a scream, a slap, a kick explodes, sometimes for no reasons. An atmosphere of arbitrariness invariably precipitates distance and withdrawal by the members, by children especially who seek to escape the madness. Finally, such a milieu is laden with deep, deep guilt emitted both by the abused "What have I done wrong?" and by the abuser "My God, what have I done?"

# ELUSIVENESS

Elusiveness as a method of communication is the direct oppositive of arbitrariness. Elusive people give responses which are vague, uncertain, or not given at all. Their responses are like that because they are quite unable to trust anyone including family. Elusiveness is the prime communicative mode of the individual beset by constant feelings of suspicion, harassment, and victimization. It is a common method among alcoholics.

Elusive people invariably engender negative responses in other people. Thus, *the alcoholic who suspects other's motives seldom gives a straight answer.* His responses are usually preceded with such qualifiers as "if", "possibly" and "I think, maybe". With the elusive person nothing is certain. Outside the family such responses can and do provoke irritability and hostility. These responses, in turn, confirm the alcoholic's basic feelings of being harassed, victimized and that people can't be trusted. Elusive people seldom come to see that they set themselves up to be treated negatively.

As the alcoholic's disease worsens the feelings of mistrust invariably become generalized toward the family members. The usual effect of this mistrust is that elusiveness becomes an integral mode of communication with the family. Now, while the elusive behaviors do indeed provoke angry responses in family members as they do in outsiders, their inevitable effect is far worse. What elusiveness does is to beget the same feelings and complementary behaviors in other family members which the alcoholic holds. In short, the feelings of distrust, harassment, and victimization become common property in the family. Vagueness and uncertainty become integrated into the family's method of interaction.

As is true with the other modes of communication elusiveness has a most unfortunate effect upon the children. They learn very quickly that by being vague, non-committal, they can't easily be blamed for anything. They can't be held accountable. Such learning, militates against learning to make commitments, to share feelings, to admit errors, and to learn responsibility for one's behaviors. These, of course, are the behaviors which make for successful living. Small wonder then, that children reared in alcoholic homes grow up bewildered and feeling emotionally isolated.

# INTELLECTUALIZATION

*Intellectualization* is the mode of communication which we use when we employ our minds rather than our emotions. It can be a valuable way of relating. Thus, via intellectualization we are able to analyze, interpret, and discuss the technical and intellectual problems which we find interesting or which impinge on our lives. At the same time, intellectualization can become destructive and does so when we use it as the exclusive or prime mode of relating to others. Why? Because such an immoderate use negates the existance of feelings—and ordinarily feelings are what attract people to people and are what make for close relationships.

*Alcoholics, especially those in the developing and middle stages of their disease, frequently use intellectualization immoderately.* Examples of these are those alcoholics who are mandated into counseling by the court for reasons of alcoholism. These counselees frequently hide behind intellectualization. The author has experienced many sessions where the alcoholic client gives long and convincing monologues on why he/she drank and why he/she had to stop and then later went out and got drunk. The point is that *when we intellectualize, we do not experience emotionally.* Only when we can blend our intellectual understanding with our emotions are we able to make meaningful commitments. Alcoholics who become accustomed to using intellectualization to explain their behavior to others and to themselves too, learn to become virtually devoid of any emotion, thereby cease to make any meaningful commitments.

Intellectualization as a mode of communication helps many alcoholics appear sophisticated, competent, and mature. The truth is they function as children because they either have not learned to integrate their feelings with their intellectual competence or they deny them altogether.

Now, among non-alcoholics the inability to integrate feelings with mental competencies, even the denial of feelings, is compensated for by a cool, calm, detached approach to problems and the motivation and ability to solve them. Such people obtain considerable status among peers for their objectivity and level-headedness. Booze effectively obviates any such compensations for the intellectualizing alcoholic for while such alcoholics are good at talking they are neither motivated, nor concerned about solving any problems, especially their own! Indeed, this type of alcoholic is generally perceived as nothing more than an inept, long-winded blow-hard. Ironically, such a perception meets the alcoholic's unconscious need to keep people at a distance.

Enablers who intellectualize the alcoholic's disease often develop a morass-like mentality about it. Thus, the process of intellectualization gives enablers the feeling that they *understand* the problem. This feeling that they understand leads to interminable discussions replete with other family members, with outsiders, and even with the alcoholic; however, note that these talks are all directed externally, on the alcoholic, and not in the least internally, on themselves, and how they are feeding into the alcoholism. In short, intellectualization provides an insulation from the problem for this kind of enabler.

# INDIFFERENCE

Indifference is usually the method of last resort in the alcoholic family. Often it comes after persons have tried any and all of the preceding methods and feel that they have failed.

Indifference in communication is usually associated with a sense of hopelessness. At the same time indifferent people are often very angry people too. They are so frequently because they have learned to relate to one or other members in a submissive way. They never learned to stand up for their rights in the family not even for their integrity. Now dominated and controlled, they turn to the last resort.

As is the case with the other methods, indifference hurts children cruelly. The message of indifference is "You are so unimportant that I don't even recognize that you are here". The emotional deprivation children experience by such behavior often results in a sense of apathy, might in the more energetic or bright ones result in much anti-social acting out. In either case the children function with a microscopic self-esteem.

People who use indifference occasionally will themselves engender much hostility in the other family members. Why? Because these occasional users of indifference are usually motivated by a need to control and manipulate. More often than not indifference is used by those in the family who are perceived as weak (i.e., the submissive enabler). Such a method precipitates loud, even abusive, responses by the dominant members (i.e., the alcoholic under the influence). In sum, the climate created by this method can be icy, can be hot, but is never enhancing.


# CASE OF THE PORTERS


When I sought to recall a family which I had in treatment which exemplified well the alcoholism methods of communication, I thought immediately of the Porters. The reason I did was not only because these modes dominated their interactions with each other but also because the Porters were one of the very few families I treated in which neither parent was addicted to alcohol. Their son Mark was the alcoholic. I first saw Mark because he was referred to me by the local District Court judge. Mark had been arrested in a road block set up specifically to apprehend people driving under the influence. Although he had been driving for only six months, Mark already had been involved in four accidents, all of them his fault.

The first session with Mark was spent discussing these accidents. What I learned was that he was very bright and articulate but had an acutely low self-esteem. This last was reflected in his innumberable self-deprecatory remarks. His favorite was, "I've got a real talent for screwing things up." At one point when I asked him how he saw himself, his quick rejoinder was "Screw-up, I'm a screw-up." When I asked him why he thought he had this self view, he replied with a puzzled look, "I don't know why but I always thought of myself like that even though everybody, the teachers and guidance counselor have always told me that I'm real smart, that I've got a high I.Q. Maybe it's true, but I never made the honor roll. It's like I said, probably it's because I'm a screw-up."

I asked him how he got along with his parents. He smiled for the first time. "O.k. but my screw-ups drive them, my father, nuts." I asked him to explain. He seemed not to want to do so as he went off on a long, unfocused discourse and talked about how his drinking wasn't any problem at all, how great his father was, and how he was going to "bust his ass" to make the honor roll the next time. I was to learn subsequently that in that discourse Mark had obliquely touched on what bothered him, had hinted at why he drank too much, why he "screwed-up" so much, why even, he had never made the honor roll. At the time I didn't know that. What I did know from my training and what I felt instinctively was that I needed to get a parental view of Mark. I needed to see his parents. He agreed to ask them to come to our next session.

Almost all people in town knew who Mark's parents were. His father Barry had his picture in the paper periodically as he was on a number of civic boards. From the write-ups I had learned that he had graduated from Princeton, had a law degree from Yale, and practiced in town. From the same blurbs I had learned that his wife Alice, had graduated from Smith College and taught English at the high school. Mark was their only child.

The Porters showed up a few minutes before the 7 o'clock appointment. They were dressed casually, Alice in a skirt and blouse, Barry in slacks and a sports shirt, and Mark in blue jeans and tee shirt.

I greeted them at the door between waiting room and office and waved them to any of the six seats. Barry and Alice sat on the three seat couch, he on one end and she on the other. Mark sat opposite them on a straight back chair. I asked them if they minded my taping the session. Mark shrugged, Alice said no, Barry asked why I wanted to. I explained that I liked to play the tape back when I was alone to see if I had missed anything important. Barry asked if he also could have access to the tapes. I nodded and even as I did I realized that I had never been asked that question before. What it meant at that point I didn't know. I was to find out.

I leaned back and looked at Mark's parents. Barry is dark haired, lean, and a little over six feet. Women, men too, if they thought about it, would say he was handsome. Alice is petite and looks like I pictured her, blond, blue-eyed, trim, and pretty—just like the wife of a prominent lawyer and civic leader is supposed to look.

Mark with his blue eyes, brown hair, and average height is a blend of the two of them.

The following excerpts were edited and cover the two and one-half month span of therapy.

### Sessions 1 Through 5

**Perez:** *I asked you both to come this evening because I felt that you might want to meet me since I'll be seeing Mark. I've* *learned that how well my adolescent clients do is affected by what goes on at home.*

**Barry:** (Looking at Perez sharply) *Are you saying we're responsible for the trouble he's in?*

**Perez:** (Shaking his head) *We're each responsible for our own behavior.*

**Barry:** *And we have to be held accountable, right?*

**Perez:** *Of course.*

**Barry:** (Smiling) *Good, I can see we're going to get along. I thought you were going to give us some of the Freudian crap that since you don't pick your mother and father you've been molded by them and you don't really have to be held responsible for what you do.*

**Perez:** (Chuckling) *I don't think that he put it quite like that.*

**Barry:** (Tone serious and hard) *Maybe not, but a major reason our criminal justice system is in the mess it is is because the emphasis is not on accountability but on understanding the why of the criminal's behavior. Say what you will that's 'cause of Freud.*

**Comments:** What I was learning fast was that Barry was threatened. Not unusual. Many men are when they are in family counseling. His request for the tapes and his remarks delivered on rather harsh tones were hostile. The hostility did not concern me too much. I felt I could handle that. What I had to avoid was being sucked into his intellectualized arguments. I learned long ago that no profit is gained in dueling intellectually with a client.

**Perez:** *There are many who would agree with you about Freud but what I'm interested in here, what I suspect we're all interested in here, is what we can do to help Mark.*

**Alice:** *We do want to help.*

**Barry:** *That's why we're here. You're the doctor. What's the prescription? Do you have one?*

**Perez:** *No, I don't have any prescription. If we all knew each other better—*

**Barry:** (Hard toned) *We're a family we know each other. I think what you're saying is you want to know us.*

**Perez:** *True. You say you're a family Barry. Are you a close family?*

**Barry:** (Quickly and looking at Alice) *Of course we are.*

**Perez:** *Are you telling me or Alice?*

**Barry:** *I'm telling everybody here.*

**Comments:** Right then I had the distinct impression that the other two Porters were constantly being told a lot. I looked at Mark who had not yet said anything.

**Perez:** (Looking in turn at all three) *What we want to do here is see what everybody's opinions and feelings are. We don't want to tell them what they are. How about it Mark do you feel you are a close family?*

**Mark:** (Shrugging) *I guess.*

**Barry:** *You guess?* (Looking away disgustedly)

**Perez:** *You're not sure.*

**Comment:** I felt Barry's hard looks pass from me to Mark.

**Barry:** *That doesn't mean much cause Mark's not sure of much.*

**Alice:** *It's his age.* (Looking at me)

**Perez:** (Softly) *Do you want to reply Mark?*

**Mark:** *It's not my age, mother.*

**Alice:** *What is it then?*

**Mark:** *It's me. I'm a screw-up.*

**Barry:** *Damnit I told you not to say that, not to refer to yourself like that.*

**Mark:** *You were saying the same thing about me just now when you said I'm not sure of much. I'm not 'cause I'm a—*

**Barry:** (Shouting and pointing his finger) *Don't you dare!*

**Mark:** (Shrugged, looking at me despiritedly)

**Barry:** (In a lowered tone quite apparently embarrassed) *Do you think we can get a handle on the problem?*

**Perez:** *We will if we all try.*

**Barry:** *What do you mean?*

**Mark:** *I think he means we have to be honest.*

**Barry:** *That's easy 'cause we're all honest. Why don't we get to why we're here. I think the whole problem is that you drink too much. If we're going to be honest, let's be honest. If you didn't drink, you'd do better in school and you'd not be in accidents. The problem is really simple. One word. Booze. No booze. No problem.*

**Alice:** *Is that the problem, doctor?*

**Perez:** *I doubt that there's only one problem here. The booze might be just a symptom of several problems.*

**Barry:** *What do you mean?*

**Perez:** *You were saying before that we all have to be held accountable for our behavior.*

**Barry:** *Yes, I believe that.*

**Perez:** *Do you always hold Mark accountable?*

**Comment:** By now I suspected he didn't.

**Barry:** *Of course.*

**Alice:** *But you don't Barry. You even had his car fixed after he banged it up, each time.*

**Barry:** *Well you always agreed to. In fact you wanted me to because you were afraid he'd drive yours.*

**Perez:** *Mark, where do you get your money for booze?*

**Mark:** Smiled and nodded toward his father.

**Barry:** (With heavy irritation) *What's your point?*

**Perez:** *What's my point Mark?*

**Mark:** *I'm getting a lot of mixed signals.*

**Perez:** (Looking at Barry) *Correct. You don't want him to drink and you give him money.*

**Barry:** *He'd get it anyway.*

**Perez:** *Probably. But by your providing it—*

**Alice:** *He's right, it's as if you're condoning it.*

**Barry:** (Angrily) *Well what about you? You give him as much money as I do. For all I know you give him more.*

**Alice:** *I never give him money.*

**Mark:** *Oh, mother, you don't because you know I've got more than enough.* (Shouting suddenly) *Besides you don't give a shit anyway, not about me, not about anything.*

**Barry:** (Shouting) *Don't you dare talk like that to your mother!* (Turning toward me) *Where are we going with all this? This is all getting out of hand. You've got me shouting. I never shout at home.*

**Alice:** *True. He never shouts.*

**Mark:** *He never says anything. No one ever says anything.*

**Perez:** (Nodding) *You don't talk to each other.*

**Barry:** *We do talk.*

**Mark:** *Dad. For God's sakes. Ma goes to her bedroom to read. You go into the den to watch T.V. and I go out. Jesus how can you say we talk!*

**Barry:** *I swear you're enjoying this.*

**Mark:** *I am.*

**Barry:** *Just like you enjoy not making the honor roll.*

**Mark:** *I don't enjoy that, no.*

**Barry:** *Then why don't you buckle down and make it?*

**Mark:** *I don't know why.*

**Barry:** *I know why!* (Shouting) *It's 'cause you're always high on something. You're operating with only half of your brain if that.*

## Summary and Epilogue

My records show that I had five more sessions with the Porters. The tapes indicate that they did not gain any insights into family dynamics and that they did not alter their attitudes or behavior toward each other. After the tenth session Barry called and cancelled the next scheduled appointment. I never saw any of them again professionally.

To understand why the Porters made little progress in therapy one needs to understand that Barry's need for status is insatiable and all-consuming. His life is dedicated toward obtaining and holding it. He pursues it by controlling all near him and by being a focal point of attention. The need is all consuming for it has to do not only with his person but also with everything associated with him, especially wife and son whom he drives to perform and to be and do for *him* as he does himself. In these terms we can understand the why of his arbitrariness.

Personally, I am no stranger to arbitrariness. My father, an immigrant, was the most arbitrary of men. Unlike Barry, however, he communicated love as much as he did arbitrariness. It was reflected in the transparent joy he found in my achievements and in the philosophical way he shrugged off my child and adolescent failures. "Life's long, Joey. You've got a lot of time to do good." Simply put, he supported me. He loved me—just because of *me*.

What Barry has always communicated is conditional love. "If you perform I will love you—no performance, no love." And the reason is always the same—to bring *him* more status and more honor.

Alice's response to Barry's arbitrariness and to his whole system of communication was to withdraw to her bedroom and read. (Barry and Alice sleep in separate bedrooms.) Essentially what Alice did was to surrender to his need to control and dominate her and Mark. In time, she became indifferent.

Mark unable because of fear to direct his hostility outwardly, directed it inwardly. Indeed his need to hurt his father was so strong that unconsciously he was willing to hurt, even destroy himself. In that context we can best understand his auto accidents and his alcoholism.

I've read about Mark a couple of times in the past year. It was on page three of our local paper under "Police Log." His offenses included being drunk and disorderly and driving under the influence. On the same page I've read about Barry's civic involvements and achievements.

All his young life Mark was victimized. He was steeped in an environment where double messages abounded and so never knew what was true. He was cowed into submission by a man whom he learned early was a giant in the community. A man who could effectively compartmentalize his tolerant, democratic outside person from his dictatorial ways at home.

Mark had an especially hard time after he entered high school. His low self-esteem guided him toward peers whom his father characterized in one session as "people of the lowest common denominator." Barry's long winded, opinionated intellectualizations only fueled Mark's burning hostility and together with his double messages and fiats enabled Mark's drinking which began in his first year of high school. Alice's apparent indifference did little to counter Barry's enabling, if anything, it facilitated it.

Mark's continued drinking led him to become elusive in his talk (Yeah, I guess, Maybe, I don't know, I'll try but—) and sneaky in his behavior. Barry talked loudly in the last sessions about how Mark had begun stowing his beer in the trunk of his car. Mark had not denied it, had not even responded, had only shrugged.

The Porter's family system of communication and the why of Mark's alcoholism are really all academic to them now because Mark's self-anger apparently intensified and he depressed into the ultimate indifference.

So on a warm, spring evening, four days before graduation from high school, Mark Porter crashed into a telephone pole in his new white convertible. The newspaper account gave no explanation as to why, only that he died alone.

**Counselor's Notes**

My best professional judgement is that

> if Barry and Alice, who knew about Mark's alcoholism, had taken time to learn all about it;
>
> if Barry had been more open-minded and less arbitrary;
>
> if Barry's and Alice's needs had centered on closeness with each other and Mark;
>
> if communication among the Porters had been *without* nagging, scolding, blaming and double-messages;
>
> if talk with Mark had been simple, honest, direct, and plentiful;
>
> if the love both parents felt toward Mark had been demonstrated periodically with hugs and kisses;
>
> if when troubled Barry and Alice had gone to each other rather than withdrawn;

if Barry's and Alice's concern for image in the community had instead been a concern for familial substance;

and if Alice had been more confrontative with both Barry and Mark and more involved in all family matters,

Mark might well be alive today.

# RECOMMENDATIONS FOR FURTHER READINGS

## Books

Black, C. (1982). *It will never happen to me.* Denver, CO: M.A.C. Pub.

Burgin, J. E. (1985). *Guide book for the family with alcohol problem.* Center City, MN: Hazelden.

Connor, R. G. (1962). *The self-concepts of alcoholics.* In D. J. Pittman and C. R. Snyder (Eds.), *Society, culture and drinking patterns.* New York, NY: Wiley, 455-467.

Costales, C. S., & Barack, P. (1984). *A secret hell: Surviving life with an alcoholic.* Ventura, CA: Regal.

Doe, J. (1978). *Alcoholism—One family's story.* Independence, MO: Herald House.

Dulfano, C. (1982). *Families, alcoholism and recovery.* Center City, MN: Hazelden.

Fajardo, R. (1976). *Helping your alcoholic before he hits bottom.* New York, NY: Crown.

Forest, G. (1980). *How to live with a problem drinker and survive.* Riverside, NJ: Atheneum.

Freud, A. (1946). *The ego and the mechanisms of defense.* New York, NY: International Universities Press.

Frey, D. & Carlock, C. J. (1984). *Enhancing self esteem.* Muncie, IN: Accelerated Development.

Kaufman, E. (1984). *Power to change: Family case studies in treatment of alcoholism.* New York, NY: Gardner.

Maslow, A. (1970). *Motivation and personality, 2nd ed.,* Chapter IV, pp. 35-58. New York, NY: Harper and Row.

Mehl, D. (1979). *You and the alcoholic in your home.* Minneapolis, MN: Augsburg.

Ohlemacher, J. (1984) *Beloved alcoholic: What to do when a family member drinks.* Grand Rapids, MI: Zondervan.

Perez, J. F. (1985). *Counseling the alcoholic,* (Part I). Muncie, IN: Accelerated Development.

Robins, L. N., Bates, W. M. & O'Neal, P. (1982). *Adult drinking patterns of former problem children.* In D. J. Pittman and C. R. Snyder (Eds) *Society, culture and drinking patterns.* New York, NY: Wiley.

Vaughan, C. (1984). *Addictive drinking: The road to recovery for problem drinkers and those who love them.* New York, NY: Penguin Books.

Woititz, J. (1983) *Adult children of alcoholics.* Hollywood, FL: Health Communications.

## Periodicals

Barnes, G. E. (1980). Characteristics of the clinical alcoholic personality. *Journal of Studies on Alcohol, 41,* 894-909.

Beckman, L. J. (1978) The self-esteem of alcoholic women. *Journal of Studies on Alcohol, 39,* 491-498.

Beckman, L. J., Day T., Bardsley, P., & Seeman, A. Z. (1980). The personality characteristics and family backgrounds of women alcoholics. *The International Journal of the Addictions, 15,* (1), 147-54.

Cutter, H. S. G., & Fisher, J. C. (1980). Family experience and the motives for drinking. *The International Journal of the Addictions, 15,* (3), 339-358.

Eastman, C., & Norris, H. (1982). Alcohol dependence, relapse and self-identity. *Journal of Studies on Alcohol, 43,* (11), 1214-1231.

Frankenstein, W., Hay, W.M., & Nathan, E. (1985). Effects of intoxication on alcoholics' marital communication and problem solving. *Journal of Studies on Alcohol, 46,* (1), 1-6.

Goldstein, G., & Chotlos, J. W. (1965). Dependency and brain damage in alcoholics. *Perception of Skills, 21,* 135-150.

Goss, A., & Morosko, T. E. (1969). Alcoholism and clinical symptoms. *Journal of Abnormal Psychology, 74,* 682-684.

Gross, W. F., & Alder, L. O. (1970) Aspects of alcoholics' self-concepts as measures by the Tennessee Self-Concept Scale. *Psychological Report, 27,* 431-434.

Harford, T. C., & Spiegler, D. L. (??). Developmental trends of adolescent drinking. *Journal of Studies On Alcohol, 44,* (1), 181-188.

Hennecke, L. (1984). Stimulus augmenting and field dependence in children of alcoholic fathers. *Journal of Studies on Alcohol, 45,* (6), 486-492.

Hesselbrock, V. M., Hesselbrock, M. N., & Stabenau, J. R. (1985). Alcoholism in men patients subtyped by family history and antisocial personality. *Journal of Studies on Alcohol, 46,* (1), 59-64.

Hoffmann, H. (1970). Personality characteristics of alcoholics in relation to age. *Psychological Report, 27,* 167-171.

Karp, S. A., Poster, D. C., & Goodman, A. (1963). Differentiation in alcoholic women. *Journal of Personality, 31,* 386-393.

Konovsky, M., & Wilsnack, S. C. (1982). Social drinking and self-esteem in married couples. *Journal of Studies on Alcohol, 43,* (3), 319-333.

McKenna, T. & Pickens, R. (1981). Alcoholic children of alcoholics. *Journal of Studies on Alcohol, 42,* (11), 1021-1029.

McKenna, T., & Pickens, R. (1983). Personality characteristics of alcoholic children of alcoholics. *Journal of Studies on Alcohol, 44,* (4), 688-700.

Milman, D. H., Bennett, A. A., & Hanson, M. (1983). Psychological effects of alcohol in children and adolescents. Alcohol Health and Research. *World National Institute on Alcohol Abuse and Alcoholism, 7,* (4).

Moos, R. H., & Moos, B. S. (1984). The process of recovery from alcoholism: III Comparing functioning in families of alcoholics and matched control families. *Journal of Studies on Alcohol, 45,* (2), 111-118.

Schuckit, M. A. (1984). Relationship between the course of primary alcoholism in men and family history. *Journal of Studies on Alcohol, 45,* (4), 334-338.

Segal, B., Huba, G. J., & Singer, J. L. (1980) Reasons for drug and alcohol use by college students. *The International Journal of the Addictions, 15,* (4), 489-498.

Usher, M. L., Jay, J., & Glass, D. R. (1982). Family therapy as a treatment modality for alcoholism. *Journal of Studies on Alcohol, 43,* (9), 927-938.

Wilks, J., & Callan, V. J. (1984). Similarity of university students and their parents; attitudes toward alcohol. *Journal of Studies on Alcohol, 45,* (4), 326-333.

# Part II

# ALCOHOLIC

# PARENTS

Chapter **4**

# COMMON DENOMINATORS OF ALCOHOLICS

The emotional health of a family is premised upon the individual health of the spouses and particularly upon the nature and quality of their relationship. The man and woman who are secure, loving, and of healthy self-esteem provide a climate which enhances each other and their children as well. When the problems of either are minor, the effect upon the other can be disturbing. When the problem is major, the effects can be devastating for both. Quite apparently, when either is alcoholic, the problems are major for both and for all others in the family.

A selected number of personality traits is common to most alcoholics. Those traits which impact most adversely upon the family members include:

1. impulsivity;

2. a low tolerance for frustration;

3. a warped perception of time;

4. an acute need for short term gratification;

5. a penchant for relationships which are short term and distant rather than close;

6. a discomfort with one's own sex;

7. a dislike or unhappiness with oneself evidenced in a disproportionate number of aches, pains, and illness; and

8. a conscience which oscillates between overscrupulousness and non-existence.

## IMPULSIVITY

A common trait among alcoholics is *impulsivity*. In large measures it is a function of the lack of confidence which they have in their own judgment. This lack of confidence continues shaky because they are constantly making bad decisions as they live and move in their alcoholic haze.

The why of their impulsivity is seldom of critical concern to family members. What they see, know, and live with is an alcoholic.

- who buys foolishly (food, clothing, furniture, whatever);

- who makes promises in

- who makes promises in an instant and then forgets them or breaks them just as instantly;

- and who invites people to visit in a genuinely sincere and charming way and, then when they do visit, the alcoholic hosts them at best indifferently, perhaps even rudely.

## LOW TOLERANCE FOR FRUSTRATION

This impulsivity is complemented by a *low tolerance for frustration*. The low tolerance can be exhibited in a variety of ways—in explosive temper tantrums, in pouting, in tears, and in excesses of various kinds, i.e., eating, smoking, and, of course, drinking.

Behaviors such as these are termed *regressive.* They are the behaviors of the emotionally inmature. If nothing else, they reveal just how emotionally stunted alcoholics really are and more importantly, *how much help they need even after they have stopped drinking.*

The major harmful effect of both impulsivity and low tolerance for frustration is that it promotes a climate of insecurity. Members never know what or when to expect things. The climate in an alcoholic family can change in an instant. A kindly pat can turn into a hard slap. A soft response begun with an approving nod can end in a harsh glare. Quite obviously alcoholics who vacillate so acutely and so instantly can only engender a host of unhealthy attitudes and behaviors in their family.

## WARPED PERCEPTION OF TIME

Many alcoholics operate with a *warped perception of time.* For many, an immediate or near event frequently is denied and seen as a long time away, i.e. a report due, a decision to be given, and so forth, this is a reason procrastination is rampant among alcoholics. On the other hand for many a long time away future event, (i.e., a talk scheduled to be given many months hence) often is a constant source of concern.

# NEED FOR SHORT TERM GRATIFICATION

A frequent corollary for this warped perception is an *acute need for short term gratification*. Both of these traits are prime reasons that alcoholics are quite unable to plan realistically for any goals. Both traits fit with the alcoholics' self-view that they are basically inept and couldn't achieve any important goals anyway. Now, when we defer gratification we invariably structure for the anxiety of doing without and possible disappointment, even failure, i.e., the person desperately wants to be independent from his parents but chooses to enroll in college rather than getting a job. Such a person often lives with a constant latent dread that he may flunk out. Alcoholics are quite unable to bind such anxiety. This is why they are quite unable to persevere toward such goals. To time confused alcoholics, to defer gratification means simply to do without—maybe forever. This is precisely why they want, what they want, and when they want it is now. In short, most alcoholics live in terms of immediate gratification. The classic feeling rationale of the typical alcoholic goes something like this, "Every day is too long. Who knows what tomorrow will bring? It may well bring disaster. I must have, shall have now whatever can get me through this day."

This insistence on gratification now is of course much like the insistence of a two year old. It is why family members ultimately come to see the alcoholic as a "big baby." This insistence, too, is what facilitates initially a protective attitude in a loving spouse, later an overprotective one. As was discussed in chapter two, this overprotectiveness conditions the alcoholic into a dependent-like infancy.


# RELATIONSHIPS—SHORT TERM AND DISTANT

*Relationships* among alcoholics can be characterized generally as being *short term and distant. By and large most alcoholics are not capable of closeness.*

Two reasons exist for this. First, alcoholics are simply not interested in other people. They are too wrapped up in and too befuddled by the mystery that is themselves. They simply do not have the energy to become involved in another person. Second, they are too fearful to let anyone into their world. This fear, in turn, promotes a host of alienating thoughts and feelings, all of which serve to keep people at a distance.

In order to maintain the facade of being a social animal both for themselves and others, alcoholics develop relationships which are at best superficial. What many do (whether they be of a passive or aggressive nature) is to develop a veneer of amiability, humor, and good fellowship. This veneer can be seen a little in the content and quality of their talk and interaction (never of a personal, self-disclosing nature). It is seen far more in the total lack of *doing* for others, in the lack of emotional involvement or concern for those whom they are so fond of calling "friends." I have seen alcoholics who were *not* under the influence react with honest indifference when told about the death of someone they have known for a lifetime.

Through my counseling I have learned that this crass indifference is usually due to the fact that most alcoholics never learned how to care for others (usually because they were never cared for themselves). I have learned, too, that many are afraid to invest in another person for fear that, if they do, they will become emotionally bankrupt. Simply, they don't feel that they could handle the potential rejection. Such a rejection, most alcoholics believe is of a very high probability.

Within the family, alcoholics continue to maintain their emotional distance but do it differently. Frequently the veneer of amiability, humor, and good fellowship is discarded. Sometimes it is replaced by a condescending, arrogant attitude, sometimes by a hypercritical, pessimistic view of self and family too. Quite apparently, both methods are effective in keeping others at a distance. Occasionally alcoholics assume a self-deprecatory stance where they cry softly or loudly about how awful they are compared to the rest of the family. Because most family members are in some measure identified with each other, this last "self-avowed black sheep" approach does little to motivate other family members to get close.

## UNCOMFORTABLE WITH OWN SEX

A disproportionate number of alcoholics, whether they are men or women, *are uncomfortable with their own sex*. Their discomfort is reflected frequently in their sense of unsureness with the opposite sex, in their fumbling and bumbling when they interact with them, and in their low and repressed sex drive.

If the alcoholic is a man, he is threatened by women, often feels inferior to them. He tends to see them as more important, more competent, and more in control. Occasionally he sees them as castrating adversaries whom he can never overcome and who ultimately will do him in. Men who grow up with this view marry women whom they can control and dominate so that they won't have to deal with their fears of what women are like. Sometimes, however, they gravitate toward the familiar, toward women who are strong and aggressive, who fulfill their unconscious understanding of what women are like. Unhappily and in typical alcoholic fashion, their choice is at the extremes. Unhappily too, in either case the choice does not bode for a happy marriage.

If a woman, the alcoholic sees men as sources of nurturance and objects to be leaned upon. To the alcoholic woman, men are all powerful and all knowing. It is for this reason that such women see their role in the marital relationship as a submissive one.

The reader might wonder why and how a man or woman with such a perception of the opposite sex would ever marry. Quite apparently they do. They do because perception of the opposite sex for most people, alcoholic or not, is largely unconscious. In sum, most people, alcoholics especially, don't know how they perceive the opposite sex. Indeed, most alcoholics, and those still only potentially, so, have a very fuzzy perception at best of their own sexuality much less understanding someone else's.

An important point to bear in mind is that only a weak self-esteem could generate such a perception of the opposite sex. The man or the woman already alcoholic, or still only potentially so, who marries tends to interact with their spouse in terms of this same perception. Their experiences in these interactions, in turn, only reinforce their already weak self-esteem.

Finally, the alcoholic's perception of the opposite sex makes a normal, healthy heterosexual relationship nearly impossible. For many this perception probably is what structures most of the problems in the alcoholic family. It is this warped perception which ultimately eradicates any giving or accepting of love between spouses. It is this warped perception which is unconsciously fed into the like-sexed child of the alcoholic.

It is this warped perception which the opposite-sex child acquires. In sum, *the discomfort which alcoholics feel with their own sex is a major reason for the emotional chaos which the alcoholic family experiences.*

## UNHAPPINESS WITH SELF

Alcoholics are not happy people. Their unhappiness most fundamentally stems from their *unhappiness with themselves.* One of the ways that many alcoholics show their unhappiness is to develop an uncommonly large number of aches, pains, and illnesses.

Among most alcoholics these aches and pains, even the illnesses, can best be understood as emotional problems converted to the body. They convert their problems to their body to obtain attention and sympathy. *Then to add to the problem, enablers with a disposition toward overprotectiveness give them as much attention as they need and more.* This attention and sympathy condition the alcoholics to become veritable hypochondriacs.

This alcoholic penchant for illness has only harmful effects. The worst probably is that illness becomes part of the family's life style. Someone's always "coming down with something" or "just getting over it" in which case they "have to take it easy and be careful" (normal activity is out). Pills are commonplace and taken with breakfast, lunch, and dinner. Pills become a food and are kept in the refrigerator.

The most unfortunate victims of such a climate are the children. As they observe and interact with enabler and alcoholic, they become supremely sensitive to sickness. They come to understand that positive rewards can be obtained from being sick. By being surrounded by such an emotional environment the children unconsciously learn to use illness to avoid confrontations, obligations, or accountability.

## CONSCIENCE
## OVERSCRUPULOUSNESS AND NON-EXISTENCE

To understand alcoholics one must understand their conscience. Invariably it operates in the extremes as it seems to *oscillate between overscrupulousness and non-existence.* My experience counseling alcoholics is that in conscience as in other aspects of their personality they function either with too much or not enough. The happy in-between, the middle of the road, is not the way of the alcoholic.

Guilt is of course the product of conscience. The bigger the conscience, the more the guilt. Alcoholics in their sober moments are persons of gigantic conscience. Their conscience seems to literally expand in reaction to their drinking and to inundate them in guilt. To anesthetize this guilt many alcoholics drink. When they sober up, they still find the guilt intense, unbearable. So they drink again.

Guilt often precipitates anger. This is especially true in alcoholics. The decisions and promises they make out of guilt are not those that they carry out cheerfully or even willingly. They resent their decisions and promises, especially those which they make expansively in the glow of their first couple of drinks. The threat of the guilt which their conscience might vent upon them is what sometimes forces them to fulfill a decision or promise. Ironic but true, right after they fulfill the promise, sometimes even in the process of doing so, they "lay the guilt trip" on the one(s) whom they promised. In so doing the alcoholic not only makes the other person(s) feel guilty but also teaches them how to inflict guilt upon others. Typical guilt promoting recriminations by an alcoholic might be illustrated by the following: "You had to make me do this (i.e., take a walk, go to a movie, visit a friend). You just had to!" "Well I hope you're satisfied now that you dragged me out here in this heat (rain, ice, snow, and so forth)." "I hope you appreciate how much this cost me (in money, time, or inconvenience)."

Intimidated and fearful the abused (spouse and especially children) reflect long and hard on whether it's worth making even mundane requests or demands of the alcoholic. More often than not they decide not to. *Dynamics such as these are why distancing occurs in the alcoholic family.*

## SUMMARY

The alcoholic's conscience structures not only for a climate permeated with guilt but also one where anger and fear abound. Ultimately the climate becomes characterized by an apathy to participate in activity as a family. Quite apparently, in such a climate love ceases.

# Chapter 5

# CASE REPORTS
# BY ALCOHOLICS

### MOMMY'S SICKNESS
#### (As Reported by the Alcoholic)

When I was asked to write this article I was nine years away from my last drink. The request produced a variety of emotions and I became very interested in exploring that part of my life.

A flash of a blond-haired blue-eyed six year old girl on a rainy Saturday morning came to mind. She is much like other six year olds; bright, precocious. Unlike most six year olds on a Saturday, she is not watching cartoons. She has been in the kitchen making Kool-Aid. A

A Concern with what is true is always a signpost of health on recovery road.

great achievement most little people are proud of. She comes into the living room with her gourmet treat and makes a profound statement: "Drink this mommy, it won't make you sick like that scotch does!" It took six months and $6,000.00 in an alcoholic treatment center to make me realize that same simple truth—"Scotch makes me sick."

Truth is what I struggle greatly with these days, but in the days of my self-inflicted madness it was the thing I dreaded facing the most. Being confronted with the destructive effect that alcoholism had on my children is probably the most difficult truth I face today. The inescapable fact is that I did it to them. I reared them in an alcoholic setting.

At age eighteen I had completed my mandatory education and supposedly was an adult ready to face the world. I didn't know that one searches for an identity, because I was busy looking for a label: good, pretty, intelligent, loved, cared-for. At age twenty I had my first child followed by two other births of healthy babies. At age twenty-eight, I began full-fledged alcoholic drinking.

Was she living more in a fantasy world than in a real one?
Was she structuring her life even then to "fall"?

Having been abandoned by my own parents at age two, I had no genuine role model of what a mother should be. I had the fairy tales and poems on Mother's Day cards. These cards said mothers were kind, caring, giving, and wonderful creatures; almost saintly and madonna-like—certainly, not drunk.

What stands out most vividly about my drinking days is how frantic they were. I was always dashing here and there, like a Keystone Cop going off in three directions at once. I'd have a sudden craving. A pizza, a sundae, an Italian grinder. I decided I wanted it. Decided I needed it and I had to have it. I got it.

Perfect example of alcoholic impulsivity!

I remember arguments too. Lots and lots of arguments with my children. I never could stand being contradicted and would never admit to being wrong especially with them. I learned in counseling that I did that because I had a "fractured self-esteem."

I remember being in bed "sick" a lot. I had migraines all the time. I realize now they were probably all part of my hangovers.

What my two younger children remember vividly is their older sister cooking meals and eating with them, taking them for walks and picnics in the backyard, and reading them bedtime stories in her bedroom. They remember Mommy "crying" and "hanging-on" to them a lot when she was drunk. I remember early in recovery being in a woman's therapy group where the topic was the inability of one particular woman to hug her child. With my ego and arrogance I stated, "Oh I hug my children all the time." The verb used by my children was "hanging-on." The reality is that in sobriety I had to learn to hug my child too. I still haven't digested the fact that I've never really been close to my kids. I'm still learning how. I'm still learning how to be a giver rather than a taker. Most women know motherhood is giving. In search for self with alcohol you become a taker of more than just a drink. Nothing is safe from your taking—friends, family, husband, or children.

*Perfect example of denial and rationalization!*

If ever there was a model adolescent, my eldest child was. She was my greatest enabler. She didn't date, party, or act irresponsibly during her high school years. She was a care-taker, dependable. Always prepared for any emergency. Life in a home with an alcoholic mother is not secure and one never knows what is going to happen. She learned to drive at age fourteen because one night when all the kids and mom went out to dinner mother got drunk, backed into four cars in the restaurant parking lot and was unable to drive. She could have called someone but she didn't want them to know about her mother, so she drove home.

I awoke the next morning in absolute panic from the blackout. How did we get home? Were the children

O.K.? If they were, who had gotten them ready for bed? What happened? I struggled out of bed, inched down the hall, peeked into each bedroom. Thank God they were safe! Then down to the kitchen to get a drink to get rid of the awful feeling! One of many, many similar incidents. Yet, I remember telling my eldest daughter, "I'm an alcoholic and I'm going to get help." Her response was, "Mom you're not that bad, don't do that." I understand now her fear of loss of her role. Today at 25 she is in the Army, a very predictable, orderly place to be. She has had several short-term relationships with very dependent men and is beginning to want answers for why this keeps happening. I'm hopeful, for she wants answers not labels, as I did.

*Her daughter had learned to deny and live with the alcoholic!*

Being married to an active alcoholic can be very lonely, confusing, and frustrating. To compensate for this my husband took as his confidante and friend, our second child, our son. There was always a power struggle for this child's attention and affection between his father and me. It was a "no-win" situation for our son, so he chose to escape. He became involved in karate, little league baseball, basketball, and other sports. He made the All-Star team and won many trophies in karate. He developed a close circle of friends with whom he spent many hours. He did anything he could to spend time away from the rest of the family because it was such a painful place to be. At eighteen he left home to live on his own. He has not been back. He is successful in terms of school, career, responsibility. He is in a relationship with his high school sweetheart. From time to time in the last two years he pops in to see his mother. There is always a connection and always a distance. There is always a Christmas visit and gifts. Some years there is even a Mother's Day card, but it is not consistent. He will not accept a commitment, for it *may* not be safe. Recently he was hospitalized for ulcers. He was told not to drink and he is finding this difficult to do. I have shared with him the fact that children of alcoholics are at high risk to develop the disease.

*Absence from reality helps denial!*

*The ulcers reflect the constant emotional conflict with which he lives!*

At sixteen my third child (a difficult position even in a normal family) became heavily involved with drugs and alcohol. She dropped out of school. I was angry as hell. Not at her. My feelings were, "Come on God, we have had our share of alcoholism in this family!" I refused to enabler her. She had to move out. Her older sister, the great enabler, took her in. Two years later she hit bottom. Today she is home. Progress is slow. She lacks confidence and needs lots of support. Sometimes I wonder if that is a true statement, or my excuse to protect her because of guilt.

*Probably a little of both.*

At fourteen the youngest child had a serious suicide attempt. As I sat by her bed in the intensive care unit and listened to a machine beep out her heartbeat, I kept asking, "Why!" "Why!" The guilt was tremendous. I had had several suicide attempts during my heavy drinking and her early childhood. Months later after much therapy, I asked her why she hadn't shared her feelings with me. Most were feelings adolescents experience during this crucial time of growth. She answered with "I was afraid you would drink." At that time, I hadn't had a drink in six years!

*Being deprived of maternal nurturance during the baby years can ultimately take a terrible toll!*

After about three years of being sober, we were sitting at the dining room table and one of the kids said, "Mom, remember the time you were drunk and we were watching Peter Pan and you thought you could fly!" My heart sank, fear and guilt was my immediate reaction, but they continued the story. "You jumped off the couch. Hit your head on the beamed ceiling and fell down. You leaped so high and hit so hard you got a concussion. Boy, did you look funny flying through the air!" They started to laugh. I started to laugh. We laughed and laughed until tears came. It was the beginning of WE.

So how do you deal with all this? First of all "I" don't deal with it. "They" don't deal with it. "WE" deal with it!

Alcoholism happened to me! The effects happened to us all. To our whole family. You see, the nineteen year marriage ended in divorce after two years of being sober. Some damage can never be repaired.

# A MOTHER WHO LEARNED TO LIVE

## (As Reported by the Alcoholic)

When I *seriously* think about me and my being an alcoholic I can't believe it happened to me. I never really *liked* the taste of any of it—I had to "acquire a taste for it." But, oh boy! did I like what it did to me—how it made me feel, and not feel.

*Again as in preceeding story, emotional deprivation during child years seems to bode for unhealthy "later" years.*

I can't remember much about growing up, like little incidents or whole stages. I can only remember feeling afraid all the time but still having to cope, to perform, to do well. My mother had a vicious temper and no one knew when she would explode. No, she wasn't alcoholic just angry all the time. My father was gentle and did little or nothing to protect me from my mother's wrath. So I lived in constant fear, I don't remember seeing and feeling much love. Not at home, not in school, not in church, nowhere.

I remember feeling very secure and able to love when I was a junior in college. I felt very good about me—a lot of people admired me and praised me for my looks and brains. I began to believe in me. I met Marty and we got married. It was during the early fifties and we were busy having kids and acquiring a house, car, things. The thing for a woman to do then was to stay home. So I did and I let all my secretarial skills evaporate. We had three kids in three years so during the mid-seventies I had to go to work to help pay for college tuitions. My husband kept badgering me to get a job and the anxiety increased. The fear the one that I'd had all my life that I would never, could ever really succeed at a job began to gnaw at me. Constantly feeling scared, I couldn't sleep. So I began to have a glass of muscatel before going to bed. Then I needed a bigger glass before I could feel relaxed so I switched to gin. God knows what happened after that. It's all a blur.

*Early emotional deprivation probably an important factor for such feelings.*

I remember being alone in the house and starting to shake. It was about 2 P.M. or so (or maybe it was 10 A.M.). Time was always a blur. The important thing I recall is walking into my bedroom at this inappropriate drinking time, dashing for the booze, gulping it down, and breathing a deep, relieving sigh when it hit me. I walked to the mirror, looked in it and said, "Jesus Christ, you're an alcoholic! Now how in hell did you get into this mess. Oh, my God, what am I going to do?"

I remember trying to stop and instead increased the amount I drank. I hid bottles everywhere. I drank morning, noon, and night. My kids (all three) were in Junior High School and doing very well. I now had another baby and she was perfect. (I didn't have a drink, not one, during this pregnancy. All the public information regarding fetal alcohol syndrome was being ballyhooed on T.V., radio, etc.) After she was born I tried so hard to control the amount, the times, and the location of my drinking. Since I hadn't had a drink for nine months, I decided I wasn't an alcoholic. I drank again. I think in nine weeks' time I made up for nine months of sobriety. I helped to build a new house, moved into it, took care of 3 adolescents and a new baby and I was tipsy, drunk, or in a blackout all the time. My booze increased from a pint to a fifth to a quart bottle each and every day. Like a baby I took a bottle to bed every night.

*The apparent "productivity" abetted her drinking.*

I remember one day about 1 P.M. I called A.A. and a man answered. I told him, "I'm an alcoholic." I cried saying those words. They meant I had no will power. They meant I would end up in the gutter. They meant I was less than human. I wept. The man asked me if I could come to the "center." I told him "no" because I had a baby napping. He then asked if he and another man could come to the house. I hung up. Two strange men coming to *my* house when I was alone confirmed my trip to the gutter. I definitely needed a drink to get through that one!! (Even as I write all this I feel there is pain, a heavy weight, a feeling deep inside me, a lump in my throat. All the pain resurfaces and again I cry.)

*No doubt about it. In our society more stigma is associated with being a female alcoholic than a male alcoholic.*

I knew the older kids knew. Sometimes I saw it in their questioning glances. At times I felt guilty, at other

76917

times hostile and flaming angry and at other times I just didn't care.

I went to soccer, basketball, tennis games, plays, teacher conferences. I did it all and I remember very little.

A Character- -istic common to the drinking alcoholic and to the one recovering too!

I had always been a very patient type of person. Suddenly I had patience with nothing and nobody. I couldn't, wouldn't put up with the least frustration. I refused to wait in lines or waiting rooms. I took to leaving my shopping cart piled high with food at the supermarket's checkout counter if I thought the line was too long. I walked out of the doctor's office if I had to wait more than a few minutes. Like it or not, sometimes I had to wait, for example at the bank to cash a check. Those times I would yell and make a scene. I remember ranting at bank tellers a lot and more than once at various bank officers.

Life was like that whenever I left the house, as if I had become injected by a mania serum. Suddenly I couldn't sit or stand still. I felt like I had to be in constant frenetic motion. The crazy frenzy left me as soon as I came back home, back to my sedative.

What finally pushed me to go to the center was a confrontation I had with Marty. I was to stop drinking or leave because "you're drinking is ruining this family and I won't let that happen" he said. I went to a motel that night. The next day I returned home to get clothes and to plead with him. I told him that I had really tried to stop but couldn't. He told me he would do anything he could to help me. Right then I knew I had all the support I would ever need. I called the center.

The "center" was located in the worst section of town. I was definitely *not* from the worse section. I couldn't conceive of walking on that street let alone into a building on that street. How strange my thinking was at that time. I didn't think anyone knew I was a drunk and at the same time I knew they knew. When I walked into the center I wasn't saved. It took several months. Finally my non-drinking alcoholic counselor asked me to take Antabuse. I knew I couldn't get through one day without a drink so he asked me not to drink for at least eight hours. When I went that day I lied and said it had been eight hours since I drank. He warned me that if any physical symptoms occurred he would rush me to the hospital. The one and only hospital in our small town. I knew if I swallowed that half pill that if I had to go to the emergency room everyone in town would know that I was a drunk. I remember hesitating. Wanting to say, "Let me die." "Don't take me there." Instead I popped the pill and swallowed it. Immediately I wished I hadn't. I was a coward. I was sick and tired of living but very, very scared of dying. I felt like such a nothing that I didn't want anyone to know me. I'd rather be dead than to be known as a drunk. I broke out in a rash, I itched, I sweated, I had trouble breathing, I paced. I got through day one. I almost didn't make it through the night. No big physical reaction, just an overwhelming feeling of anxiety and dread. The center opened at 9 A.M. I flew there at 9:01 A.M. I paced... paced...paced. Day two passed, then days three and four.

*That popping of the pill was a manifest, concrete resolution to herself that she really wanted to recover!*

What pushed me to finally stop drinking was a major confrontation with my counselor after one of my "slips." He said he knew I was still drinking and soon I would start drinking on the job. (I had gotten a job about three months previously.) I liked my job and the people I met there. One evening I began shaking at work. I couldn't wait to get to my car to have a gulp of gin and I knew my counselor was right. I couldn't keep it at bay any longer. It was a lion devouring me. I had to stop or kill myself. Nobody likes a drunk but everyone feels sorry for a suicide victim. The problem was that I was too scared to die!!

The hardest things for me were to drive by a liquor store and to live through the nights. I knew where every liquor store was located. I clenched the car's steering wheel everytime I drove by one. About three weeks after practically living at the center I drove by a liquor store and I didn't realize it was looming there in the corner of my eye. You know what I wanted to do? I wanted to stop the car in the middle of this busy street, jump out, and yell to the whole town, "Free at last! Oh, my God, I'm free at last."

About one year after I had stopped drinking I came home from work in a very silly mood. My elder 17 year old daughter very cautiously asked if I was drinking again. I was furious with her and it hurt inside me. This episode was another milestone. I realized I had hurt many other people and also that it would take a long time maybe forever, for my family to forgive and to trust me. But it was my own doing that caused the suspicion. It may never happen, nevertheless it was worth trying to recapture their esteem and love.

*Such an admission reflects a healthy self perception.*

Much of my life is forgotten. The early years were lost by fear, the middle years by booze. Perhaps the later years I'll remember because I'm loving again. I remember stating earlier that saying "I am an alcoholic" meant many negative things. Now I'm *mostly* glad that it happened. I'm a much better human being because of it. I'll tell you something though. I wish I could have learned from a dream instead of from a nightmare. I have been eleven plus years without booze. It just dawned on me, learning by living is the best.

## A FATHER DESENSITIZED
### (As Reported by the Alcoholic)

*Procrastination common to the alcoholic is common to the recovering alcoholic too! Stopping drinking does not*

When Dr. Perez asked me to write this two months ago I said, "Sure! Why not? Glad to!" and I meant it. When he told me that I could take two months to do it if I needed that long, I told him that I'd have it ready a lot sooner than that. The two months and then some have gone by and I'm just beginning it. It's been like that all my life. Time slips like water through my fingers. I wink my eyes and a month has passed. I'm forty-two years

old now and time still is very much of a mystery to me. I
wonder if it is to everybody else.

*radically alter the personality.*

I taught French in high school for thirteen years. I
didn't like teaching. I never did. I hated the kids. They
shit all over me. Right from the first day I had a
discipline problem. My first principal told me that my
problem was that I was not strong enough. What he
really meant was that I was a weak man. I hated him but
I was scared of him. That's why I took that crap from
him. I guess I was a very scared guy because I took crap
from everybody. My shrink said that it was all probably
due to a low self-esteem. It it was, then mine had to be
below my toes. The reason I got tenured was that the
principal never wrote me up, never told the School
Board about me. He had a heart attack the week before
the School Board passed on the tenure applications. A
week later he died. I figure he must have found out that
I got tenured.

You might wonder why I even wanted to teach if I
hated it. Simple. I had a wife, a month old baby, a
mortgage, and a cat. Besides all that, I didn't know
what else I could do for a living. What do you do with a
major in French? As a senior in college and before I met
my wife, I took the Foreign Service exam and flunked.
No surprise. I knew I would. Even though I learned to
read and speak it, I can't understand it. Much of the
exam had to do with comprehension. Anyway I got the
teaching job. Nobody else applied.

I started drinking like a drunk the afternoon after I
put in my tenure application. I couldn't bear the anxiety
of waiting to hear. After I got the "good news" I stayed
drunk for three days. My wife Linda in those first
months of our marriage and while she was still pregnant
took care of me and protected me. She was my enabler
par excellence. Anyway she called me in sick for those
three days.

*A common beginning for alcoholism — drinking to escape anxiety.*

I developed a very careful schedule for buying my
beer. I never hit the same package store twice in one

month. I did all my drinking at home. I went right there after buying my booze. My drinking began at four o'clock and ran to about ten when I would stagger to bed. Weekends and holidays it began about 11:30 A.M. Once I started I just continued until I passed out, usually watching T.V.

*Despite impressive insight, drinking continued. This is common. Truth was, he was not motivated; he saw no reason to stop drinking!*

Except for the three days lapse when I "celebrated" my being tenured, I never missed another day of school. I'm convinced today that that three day spree happened because I was scared and depressed. I saw being tenured as a sentence to a vocational hell.

I'm sure my alcoholism began to show. Until my tenure I'd always weighed about 160. I ballooned out. Within a year of my "serious drinking" (that was my term for it) I weighed close to 190. I also ate like a pig. My newly developed beer belly helped me look like that pig. I must have really looked like hell on those days that I forgot to shave. There were a lot of those.

At lunch one time in the school cafeteria I was on one side of a partition eating alone when I heard one secretary talking to another about me. I never forgot her comment. "Everytime I see that man I want to put him in a Maytag washing machine." I remember finding some kind of perverted delight in her disgusted tone. I didn't increase my showers.

Looking back I find it amazing that no one at school ever commented to me about my appearance. My wife didn't either. She didn't seem to notice my drinking. For that matter she no longer noticed me at all. The baby was born. Right from the day she came home from the hospital, she was completely wrapped up with the baby.

See, Linda and I had to get married. I never loved her. I certainly never wanted to marry her. I had to. I was brought up in a strict Baptist home. There were a lot of rules in my house. All don'ts. Don't drink. Don't smoke. Don't swear. Especially don't screw. My father, mother too, were the types who punctuated every sentence with a hallelujah and finished every paragraph of their lives with a bibilical quote. That's exaggerated but only a little bit. Anyways if I hadn't married Linda, I would have spent the rest of my life marinating in my guilt.

What was ironic about the whole pregnancy was that I was never much with girls. I never dated one in high school, in college either. Girls made me nervous. No brag just fact. Linda chased me. She was on a church committee with my mother. I met her in my house. We went out a couple of times. She was the only girl I ever went out with. I went out with her because I figured I was supposed to. Boys went out with girls. She seemed very receptive to my fumbling sexual advances. In fact, I'd say she was more aggressive that way than I was. It's interesting after she got pregnant she seemed to lose all interest in sex. What I realize now is that she wanted the baby, not me! I was used.

*Such bewilderness with the opposite sex is not uncommon among potential alcoholics.*

*This feeling of being used fuels the alcoholic's need to continue to drink.*

My life began to change a little over two years ago when Linda's parents were killed in an auto accident. A week later she walked out on me with our 14 year old and went to live in her parent's house. The divorce became final six months later. She had asked for nothing, not even child support. I wasn't hurt only relieved.

The central theme of this story was supposed to be my experience as an alcoholic parent. I can't do that because the truth is that I don't have much experience as a parent. I'm a parent but only biologically. I never was a father to my daughter Brenda. I never fed her, diapered her, played with her. I never tucked her into bed or kissed her good night like you see on T.V. or in the movies. Like I said, I never did as a parent. Funny, but I never felt I had to. Linda never asked me to and I never wanted to. It's an awful thing to say but it's true. I always saw my daughter as Linda's child, not mine. She raised her, not me.

*Such emotional isolation from the rest of the family is typical among alcoholics.*

I never developed any real affection for her because I never had any experiences with her. We lived in the same house but we didn't have much to do with each other. I came home from school, went into the den and watched T.V. She stayed near her mother. I guess I was kind of a phantom for her, there in spirit but not really there. My experience as a parent taught me that you really aren't, if you're alcoholic. It may sound awful but it's true, I'm not especially sorry about what I missed because I just don't know what I missed. I know this all sounds a little insensitive, and it is. It is because that's what alcohol does. It desensitizes. That fact explains my alcoholism to me better than anything else. I *wanted* to be desensitized to being a husband and a parent. That's why I was drunk during my whole marriage and all of Brenda's life.

There is still much anger in the man and the sense of victimization ( of being used) abides in him But he has it well controlled. And, importantly, he continues in his sobriety.

Anyway I stopped needing drink that day Linda and Brenda moved out. My need to be desensitized and insulated from them and my whole life just plain evaporated. Suddenly I didn't want to be drunk anymore. I went to see Perez. I learned a lot of things about myself. Basically what I learned was that I can be in control of my life if I want to be. I learned that I didn't have to be a teacher if I didn't want to be. I did it. I quit teaching. Today I'm working as a computer programmer. It suits me. I'm always in control. Unlike kids, computers never shit on you.

## GRATEFUL DAD
### (As Reported by the Alcoholic)

As I walked along the street on a September evening with my son, recently turned 16 years old, I pointed out the beauty of the sky.

"But it's the August sky you like best at night, isn't it?" he asked.

He was right. Years ago, in the summers before the divorce, I used to love the August nights on Nantucket when the moon was full and low and shooting-stars criss-crossed the sky. But I was surprised that he would know this and I said so.

"Don't you remember," he said, "how you used to come in and wake us up when we were kids and make us go out and look at the sky in August?"

I said that I remembered but, in truth, I did not.

"You kids must've thought I was crazy," I said.

He looked at me and smiled the kind of smile that conveys understanding and a bit of forgiveness. He was now almost my height and he was a polite and modestly self-assured star athlete and an "A" student, well adjusted and at home both among kids his own age and among adults.

"No," he said, "we didn't think you were crazy."

I was grateful for that kindness and I dropped the subject. It had been nearly five years since I had taken a drink of alcohol and often during that time of sobriety I had wondered just what my children really did think of me. But despite my occasional resolve to find out, the question always seemed inappropriate when I was with them. What does one ask, "So, anyways, how'd it feel to have a father who was a drunk?"

My relationship with my son and daughter was like my relationship with everybody I knew. It was distant. Never had I been able to talk with either about feelings and emotions and this inability has always loomed large as a void in my life. Their mother could do so. I recall the persistent sense of loss I would feel each night when they would go to her and hug and kiss her, then turn to me and from a respectable distance bid me goodnight. It was as though I was somehow crippled or handicapped —wanting very badly to express my affection both verbally and physically while at the same time being incapable of even the simplest gesture. How could they be

*The inabil-
ity to emote
reflects the
confusion
we have
about our-
selves. Also,
this inabil-
ity may be
a reason
so many
alcoholics
drink —"to
loosen up".*

expected to understand the true depth of my feelings for them when even I could not understand my failure to show them? It seems that I tried to preserve my sanity by denying my own feelings, and the ultimate tragedy was that I failed both at admitting my feelings and at denying them. That doesn't leave you much.

What it leaves you is....well....wondering. That's what I've been doing during the years since the divorce. I wonder. I wonder why I've not been able to emit or relate to the emotion of others and my children's especially. Sometimes I think it's due to the curse of us alcoholics, a sense of inferiority that permeates our very soul. The shrinks call it a low self-esteem. We alcoholics live with the notion that we are different, that we are a lower form of people. To too many of us our disease is a sign of our unworthiness. that we don't feel worthy enough to share our love is the best sign of the sense of that unworth. Besides what normal person can really understand how and what we feel? Why would they ever want to? What do we really have to offer anybody? Even our children? These awful thoughts, this awful wondering still plagues me.

*It may
have been
a need to
prove his
masculin-
ity to the
world.*

I don't remember what fantasy of fatherhood I was entertaining when, after a couple of years of marriage, I forced the idea of having our first child on my reluctant wife. However I do recall that the idea was entirely my own and only months of demanding and arguing caused her to relent. She cried upon learning that she was pregnant and they were clearly not tears of joy.

Years later, at the time of the divorce, I would learn from her the source of her reluctance. "I knew it was a mistake to marry you even before the wedding," she would confess, "but things had gone so far it was just too embarassing to back out."

What she knew even then was that there was only one constant in my life, constant drinking. Beyond that reliable trait I was given to all manner of impulses, unpredictable behaviors and moods. I had begun a year after the marriage and a year before the arrival of our daughter to medicate my anxiety, my depression, and my fears with gin and to fuel my drives and fantasies with it as well. She was a remarkably stable person, very steady and reliable, and her senses warned her, darkly, of the potential disaster of sharing parenthood with me.

From the very beginning alcohol would insinuate itself between me and my children. This first happened on the very day that I was to bring my first-born, my daughter, home from the maternity ward. The hospital had scheduled the discharge for anytime after 10 A.M., and I had arrived at about that time. As I entered the hospital lobby I could feel the ghostly fear, the anxiety that plagues the alcoholic begin to stir within me. I boarded the elevator and as I rose to the maternity floor the fear erupted into panic, as I knew it would, as it always had for the past year. I was trembling for want of a drink and I was certain that I might go insane if I tried to function without one.

Without getting off when the elevator arrived at the maternity floor I pushed the button to return to the lobby. Once there I hurried back to the parking lot and drove to a package store where I purchased a half pint of vodka, still believing it was oderless. I drove around for nearly an hour, drinking the alcohol and allowing this "medicine" to relax me and control my mood. All the while, as I drove and drank, my wife and infant daughter waited, fully clothed, to be taken home.

Finally satisfied that I was in control of myself, which is to say finally half drunk, I returned to the hospital and went directly to the maternity floor. But even then I had miscalculated the amount of gin necessary to deal with fatherhood. I still trembled as the nurse tried to hand my daughter into my arms. I refused to take her for fear I'd commence to shake violently and drop her. An experienced nurse solved the dilemma by simply thrusting the infant into my arms and withdrawing.

*The actual sight of the baby terrified him because it made his parenthood with all the attendant responsibilities and accountabilities more real, actual and terrifying, as he "knew" he could never meet them.*

Eighteen months later, while suffering some common childhood ailment, my daughter's fever reached such a degree that she went into a febril convulsion. My wife was with her in the nursery when it happened at about 11 P.M. on a bitter cold night in February. I was down the hall, lying in bed reading, dressed only in boxer shorts. When I heard my wife scream I ran to the nursery and seized the baby off the bassinette. Somehow mindful that precautions must be taken to prevent a person having a convulsion from chewing their tongue, I thrust the index finger of my right hand into my daughter's mouth, and she clamped down upon it with her four teeth, two on the top and two on the bottom. I phoned my father for transportation to the hospital, since my wife was paralyzed with fear. When he arrived I flew out of the house and into the car with her still cradled in my arms. Upon arriving at the emergency room I created a substantial disturbance in demanding better services for the baby than were being provided. Short of being taken into custody by hospital security guards, I calmed down and took a seat in the waiting room.

*The behavior described here was a response to an over-scrupulous conscience —overscrupulous because of the isolation he maintained from parental concerns while under the influence.*

It was then that I felt cold vinyl on my back and my legs and realized that I had been out in the February weather of minus ten degrees with no clothes on other than my shorts. Later, about 3 A.M., I would feel pain for the first time in my finger, which had been broken.

All of this occurred when I was quite sober. Yet, the following day, try as I might, I could not force myself to enter the hospital and journey up to the second floor to pediatrics to visit my child. I was obliged to first go to a bar to drown the awful guilt. I remember later going up the elevator to make my visit but I don't remember seeing her.

I functioned like that. I functioned like that throughout her and my son's childhood. I was never a father to them during the first decade of their lives. I try to be now during their teen years. I visit them a lot. My long bout with alcoholism and the subsequent sobriety has made me more introspective, more silent, and much more of a listener. When we visit, my kids and I, I hurt much inside for the years I missed but I marvel too at the continuing miracle of my recovery. God, I'm grateful for that! Grateful especially that I can see and appreciate the beauty and love of my children.

*The hurt is realistic and mercifully helps to assuage the guilt.*

## Notations

The four stories are very different from each other, two are about mothers, two about fathers. Nevertheless, there are some very important commonalities. All of them explain and graphically describe the pain of being an alcoholic parent. All of them, too, are about the courage to change, to become sober, and to face the pain of sobriety and thereby, the pain of the emotional dysfunctions which precipitated the alcoholism in the first place. More importantly, what these stories teach us is that sobriety to be lasting must be accompanied by change in life style.

The real importance of these stories, however, lies not in their revelation of courage to change, important and admirable as that might be. Rather it lies in the hope which they exemplify to those of us, alcoholic and non-alcoholic who continue to struggle and cope in an alcoholic family. Their message is clear. Alcoholism can be overcome!

# Part III

# CHILDREN

# OF

# ALCOHOLICS

# Chapter 6

# COMMON DENOMINATORS

### in

### CHILDREN
### OF
### ALCOHOLICS

Children who grow up in alcoholic families grow up emotionally deprived. Sometimes they are reared in situations where the climate is explosive. Temper tantrums, sudden and unpredictable happen, seemingly for no reason. Here people scream, cower, and cry. Sometimes the climate is just the opposite, so undisturbed that the children learn to live in an environment which could be described as tomb-like; one where no talk, no communication occurs and where members function in isolation and keep secrets from one another. Sometimes the climate is in between these extremes. Even so in these "middle climates" the children are often abused verbally and/or physically and if they are not abused themselves, they see other members so abused they come to understand that hyper-criticism and nagging are viable and legitimate ways of interacting.

Promises, they come to learn, are not necessarily binding as they may or may not be kept.

Climates such as these promote insecurity. Climates such as these promote a sense of isolation and of never having been loved. Climates such as these promote a poor sense of self worth. *Children of alcoholics come to negate the worth of their own love and feel unworthy of anyone else's.* For many the giving and taking of love become a mystery. The feelings of insecurity, the ineptness with love, and the low self-esteem are the major reasons that these children as adults exhibit a veritable host of debilitating personality traits. Chief among these are

1. a constant need for approval;

2. a low ability to persevere;

3. an inability to trust;

4. unreliability;

5. a tendency to lie a lot and often for no reason;

6. an attraction to pain;

7. vacillation;

8. an inability to get close to others;

9. a tendency to become involved in relationships which are based upon pity, not love;

10. a terror of being evaluated; and

11. a frantic way of life.

Before proceeding please note that my intention is not to even suggest that the children of alcoholics are all alike. Quite the contrary. Like their parent alcoholics and enablers they are seen here as all different from one another. The previously listed traits and descriptions which follow can best be understood as characteristics in their unique personalities. In some children of alcoholics, some of these characteristics are dominant, in other children barely discernible, and in still others some of these characteristics do not exist at all.

# CONSTANT NEED FOR APPROVAL

Adult children of alcoholics tend to have an acute and *constant need for approval*. More often than not this stems from the emotional paradox in which many were steeped in childhood. They grew up in sharply contrasting emotional extremes. One parent (usually the alcoholic) was indifferent or rejecting, while the other one, out of misguided good intention to balance the emotional equation, was studiously over solicitious, if not overprotective. A worse situation (more common too) for such a person was to live a childhood where the same parent(s) (alcoholic) vacillate(s) between superabundant love, attention, and caring and icy indifference and/or hostile rejection. Behavior at both extremes of the emotional continuum is, of course, common among alcoholics as it is a function of the guilty conscience and inebriation.

*The constant need for approval can be, often is, channelized in doing for others.* The gratitude and recognition they receive fuels them to continue to do for and to serve others throughout their lives. This is especially true among those who never become themselves alcoholic. They seldom, if ever, examine the why of their constant need to do and serve others. Their frenetic activity is the alternative they choose to self-examination. It has a fringe benefit too, as it salves their conscience, albeit never fully. Their conscience, in most cases, is oversized and is the reason they make so many decisions out of guilt and not out of choice. A person such as this is, of course, the ideal candidate for the role of enabler. As a result many do become so. They do because like most people they gravitate consciously or unconsciously toward those whose ways are familiar and which they feel they understand. If nothing else, potential enablers do indeed understand the ways of the budding alcoholic. Therefore, often they marry one.

A most unfortunate effect among those with an oversized conscience is that they feel guilty all the time. Their guilt may be such that they seldom take a stand on anything, even if their integrity is involved. What they believe depends upon to whom they are talking. This is true especially with strangers. Such a submissive approach results inevitably in a loss of self-respect and the respect of others. The anger engendered in the child of the alcoholic by such submissiveness by those outside the family (and there is usually a lot) is often displaced upon family members. It is a reason why there is so much nagging, hypercriticism, and physical abuse in the alcoholic family.

# LOW ABILITY TO PERSEVERE

*Children of alcoholics have a low ability to persevere* in most activities even those which they enjoy. In those activities which are unappealing or which are threatening their ability seems virtually nonexistent. As college students their class attendance is at best spotty, frequently downright poor. If they have chores at home, their style is to do them sporadically, not at all, or frantically. Most projects, even minor tasks, seem to be finished with little enthusiasm, often grudgingly. They change their jobs often and are the ones who suffer "burn out" most. In short, achievement and striving for success are not prime motivating factors in their lives. They are not because many *children of alcoholics are plagued by the latent but constant fear that they are going to fail whatever the endeavor, project, or work.* This is especially true when they are confronted by new tasks and fulfilling obligations. Their response invariably is to procrastinate. Their emotional rationale seems to be, "If I don't try, I can't fail." Their inability to persevere and their penchant for procrastination can best be understood as a defense against lowering further their already pitifully low self-esteem.

# INABILITY TO TRUST

Children of alcoholics are *unable to trust.* Trust is learned in a stable home, one where the child can predict with a high degree of accuracy what's going to happen. The alcoholic home filled as it is with acute emotional vacillations and broken promises quite apparently militates against such learning. The children of alcoholic families emerge from childhood distrustful and suspicious of people. Their distrust costs them much. Because of it they are unable to get emotionally close to others. As children, they are unable to identify with adults and peers and thereby enrich their personalities.

This inability to identify with others is the reason that during the childhood years these children appear so bland and apathetic in both appearance and disposition. The blandness and apathy seem to evaporate during adolescence and adulthood but in truth are merely veneered beneath the social sophistication which comes with an increase in age. The core suspicions and distrust learned in childhood are very much there. *These suspicious and distrust are the prime reasons for the poor quality of their interpersonal relations.* The simple truth is that people can't get close to others if they can't trust. Children of alcoholics can't trust.

## UNRELIABLE

The children of alcoholics tend to be *unreliable*. This unreliability is a function of their low self-esteem. Self-esteem influences performance and mightily, i.e., if we think we're good, we perform adequately. A disportionate number of children of alcoholics believe that they are inadequate. Because of this self-view, they resort to the emotional rationale previously noted, "If I don't try, I can't fail." The result of these unfortunate cause and effect dynamics is that they present themselves as unreliable. That they do so is not of special significance to them because they grew up with unreliability. In most instances being surrounded by one or more unreliable persons was an integral part of their childhood milieu. As adolescents and adults they do like most people do, they mirror the behavior with which they are familiar and which they understand. Like most people, too, *they are far more concerned with maintaining some semblance of respectability in their self-esteem than they are in projecting an image of reliability.* In their view they have to do that if they are to function at all.

## LIE FREQUENTLY

Children of alcoholics *tend to lie a lot and often for no reason.* Several reasons exist for this. As children they spent much of their lives in fantasy to escape the chaotic, harsh reality of their real world. Many learned to find so much reward in their world of imagination that their fantasy lives became as important to them as the real world. For some, it became more important. For all of them *fantasy became an integral defense for the harsh reality which they continue to perceive in adolesence and adulthood.* To mitigate that harshness, they invariably blend their fantasies with reality. The effect of all this fantasizing is to develop a distorted perception of self, of reality, and simply, of what's true. More often than not, they come to believe the reality which they perceive even though it is a blend of their own imagination.

For these reasons children of alcoholics view all their lies as "white" lies and, if something is not exactly as they said it was, they feel justified in feeling and believing that it should be! Most of them are quite oblivious of the fact that when they blend fantasy with reality they are really telling themselves and others that reality and truth are really not important.

## ATTRACTION TO PAIN

Many children of alcoholics seem beset with an *attraction to pain*. The why of this is not difficult to fathom if one keeps in mind the fact that conscience is a very real and major factor in the alcoholic family. It is usually evident, if not dominant, in all intra-familial interactions. More often than not conscience is the critical determinant for the decisions made, both major and minor. In families such as these, conscience literally inundates the children with guilt, guilt which precipitates the need they have to punish themselves. Punish themselves they do with worry, useless anxiety, imaginary ailments, accidents, a constant sense of unworthiness, and so forth. Bizarre, but true, in the view of some of those reared and steeped in the crazy dynamics of alcoholism, such punishment is a kind of penance to atone for the original sin of being born into an alcoholic family. Thus, *children of alcoholics gravitate toward pain because they find that feelings of hurt salve their feelings of guilt.*

The most salient manifestation of their need to punish themselves is probably reflected in the harshness with which they judge themselves in all that they do and especially in the constant denigration of their physical looks. They are never pleased with how they look. If nothing else, this constant displeasure reflects the basic sense of loathing with which they live.

## VACILLATION

Children of alcoholics tend toward *vacillation*. This is not surprising because most were reared by role models who were indecisive, indifferent, and of a low self-esteem. Most of these children became what they were exposed to.

Decision-making for them is a painful experience, filled with much doubt and even more dread. To make decisions, they feel, is to reinforce the basic self-understanding they have that their judgement is terribly poor. If they do not make decisions, such reinforcement can not occur. So they vacillate.

What is ironic about vacillation is that it is both a product and a precipitator of anxiety. Thus, vacillators who are too anxious to make a decision only increase their anxiety by not doing so when finally caught between the proverbial "rock and hard place." At that point their anxiety is such that their judgement may indeed be poor and their decision faulty. In this way they realize their basic self-understanding about their ineptness to make decisions. What should be noted, too, is that via this self-fulfilling prophecy they also structure the anxiety for the next decision they have to make.

## EMOTIONALLY DISTANT FROM OTHERS

The children of alcoholics find it *difficult to get emotionally close to others*. This is not surprising because the ability to get close, to love is founded on learning feelings of trust. Such feelings are learned best, most easily during the childhood years.

Now, if as children we are not exposed to closeness but to much rejection and indifference, as children are in the alcoholic family, our sense of trust is developed poorly if at all. Why? Because when we let ourselves get close to others, when we love, we open ourselves up to potential hurt. We *trust* that our love will not be rebuffed but returned.

If the love we give as children is returned in kind or even more bountifully, we learn to trust, we learn to love, we learn to get close. Children of alcoholics learn early in life that they can not trust because they never saw much love between their parents. More often than not, they themselves were the object of a love which was at best sporadic and unpredictable. In short, *what they learned in childhood was that the chance of being hurt was very strong if they got emotionally close*. Unfortunate but true, throughout their lives most of them are not willing to risk that chance.

# RELATIONSHIPS RESULTING FROM PITY

Many children of alcoholics, though unable to get close, still develop relationships with others. However, these *relationships are not based upon love but upon pity.* These relationships then are not relationships of give and take, are not peer-like but are characterized by emotionally sophisticated condescension.

To be in a relationship where one is the pitier is not threatening. One can feel kind and noble about oneself in such a situation and any demands made upon the pitier can or can not be met without guilt. Love, especially peer love, is something else. Peer love necessarily involves not only the sense of trust, already noted, but also a healthy self-esteem, a feeling that one has something of emotional worth to offer the other person. Quite apparently, peer-love means being loved, accepting the love of another. Such acceptance involves obligation, i.e., one has to pay love back. Right here is a critical rub for the children of alcoholics. They are acutely threatened by obligations of any kind. Paying back love is threatening indeed. To obviate such an occurrence and *to still feel that they are giving of themselves, they seek out, find, and relate to people whom they can pity.* In this way they are able to deny their inabilities to love in a peer and meaningful way.

# TERROR OF BEING EVALUATED

The children of alcoholics live constantly with *a terror of being evaluated.* To most of them, to be evaluated means to be demeaned because they believe they will be found wanting. They go to extreme, sometimes self-defeating lengths, not to be evaluated. If college students, they are emotionally paralyzed by every test they have to take. They procrastinate about submitting papers on time and thereby often have grades lowered. As workers, they tend to gravitate toward lower paying, fringe-benefited, bureaucratic-like jobs which are not periodically evaluated. They prefer such jobs to those where the compensation is higher but where productivity and competence are periodically evaluated.

Although children of alcoholics seldom get into positions of prime leadership, responsibility, and accountability, they do sometimes rise into minor or middle managerial type jobs. In such positions *they live with the constant dread that they will be found unsuitable if not inept.* To protect themselves from any such eventuality they become clerks par excellence. They keep minutes of all meetings and then distribute the minutes immediately afterward if the agenda was not personally threatening, much later when memories have become fuzzy or blended if even the slightest threat to them was present. In these ways they are able to color what transpired and put themselves in a more favorable light. Such behavior is of course not peculiar to the children of alcoholics but is indeed common in any hierarchical structure be it industrial or governmental. Nevertheless, *the need to protect one's derriere is a most acute and compelling one for children of alcoholics.* It is not, however, their only method of dealing with the constant threat with which they live on the job. *The other way is namely, not to take a definitive stand or any stand where one might become the focal point of attention and possibly be wrong.* To be wrong to the child of an alcoholic raises the spectre of being demeaned, disciplined, or dismissed. This is not so likely to happen if they never take a stand. So they don't. This elusive response to threat (see Chapter 3) is learned from an alcoholic parent or enabler. A manifest purpose of elusiveness is to prevent a low self-esteem from being lowered further. Ironically it does just the opposite. More often than not elusive people come to think less and less of themselves precisely because they don't know what they believe.

## FRANTIC WAY OF LIFE

Children of alcoholics lead *a frantic way of life*. The reason for this is a function of their over-sized conscience and the super-abundant guilt which it precipitates. As we have noted in various contexts, love is a rare commodity in the alcoholic family. One of the unfortunate effects of that rarity is that children learn that, if they are to obtain any at all, they must do, act, work, and contribute.

*A grateful glance from a harried enabler mother or a bleary-eyed alcoholic father is usually enough to cause an emotionally deprived six year old to continue doing the dishes every night throughout his/her child life and to assume other duties far beyond their child-like competence.* What these children learn is that, if they want even the tiniest crumb of emotional acceptance, they have to earn it and that they have to do so with an undue expenditure of effort too. Very often their efforts go unrewarded. Even the crumbs are withheld. Still they persevere. They do because they see no alternative. With the advent of adolescence the indifference and the sporadic crumbs of the alcoholic and/or enabler take their toll. Their perseverance to contribute, indeed their perseverance for whatever, ends. Their constant frenetic activity does not. Productivity is not the issue for them anymore, just activity. In this way, they are able to justify their existence to themselves.

# Chapter 7

# CASE REPORTS
# BY CHILDREN
# OF ALCOHOLICS

## SON OF AN ALCOHOLIC MOTHER
### (As Reported By The Son)

I feel angry being the son a an alcoholic. I am an alcoholic and I believe that I would not have gone through the hell I did if my mother was not an alcoholic. Life is hard enough when one is healthy, to be afflicted with this disease makes *everything* in life so much more difficult. This disease often perverts my perception which causes me to structure situations that will sometimes greatly increase my chances to fail, feel guilty, be rejected, or just make my life more difficult. All

*The sense of victimization is realistic, is strong, hopefully will weaken with age.*

this I believe because my mother is an alcoholic. I feel damned angry sometimes, especially when my own disease is acting up.

Only after twenty months of sobriety am I beginning to feel and understand things. I believe that for the first time in twenty-seven years I am able to look back at my mother's behaviors and realize that many of her behaviors occurred because of her drinking. I never knew this until the end of her drinking, that she behaved the way she did because of booze. In short, I never associated my mother's confusing, double messages with her drinking—again until the very end of it. Try to imagine how that feels, to be subjected to confusing behaviors and not know that you are confused. That may sound weird, but it may not if you are the child of an alcoholic.

*Bewilderment is an integral aspect of growing up in an alcoholic home.*

My mother on many occasions with a smile handed me money like it was lettuce leaves; then five minutes later, she would be storming, raging about how angry "us kids" made her. On one particular occasion, I asked her if I could have a dollar to go to the store. She handed me approximately seven one dollar bills. Both my parents always made it clear in my house that money didn't grow on trees. My mother's nonchalant regard for money in these instances confused me, scared me and although it was her behavior, it made me feel guilty. However, being the practical thirteen year old I was, I knew this opportunity would not happen often. I took the money, stashed it, and laid awake nights (until I spent the money) feeling guilty and wondering about my mother's behavior, her glassy eyes, swaying stance as she handed me, "all that cash".

*Such behavior promises insecurity because it is so terribly instant, unpredictable.*

I really didn't know she was drunk, just a little different, but not enough to ask, "What's the matter?" I was naive. I can see now that I was angry and frustrated but I didn't *know* that. I was this way for many years. I was because she always made me wonder, she always made me guess and invent explanations for her behavior. To live through that for as long as I did was horrible (and I really only remember seven months of her drinking). To be subjected to sick behavior and not see it as sick, to not be told that it's sick caused me to get sick. Honest communication in our house stopped. Consistency stopped. Health stopped. To write about this even now causes the anger to be stirred up in me and I feel, very simply, pissed off! Her alcoholism caused mine! Jesus!

I remember my mother being grossly obese. I remember feeling ashamed of her. I wouldn't want to play on our family blanket when we went on vacation to the beach. In fact I would try to avoid that whole area of the beach.

I specifically remember one incident one summer at the beach when my mother betrayed my trust. My middle school principal shared "our beach." I had told my mother a nickname I had made up for her. My mother I *Whom can you trust if you can't trust your own mother?* know now was probably a little drunk, anyway she told her my nickname. I couldn't believe it, for me at that time it was a big thing. I was still in *her* school. God, I was so embarrassed! Not only that, but again, I felt betrayed and that was one thing that was a cardinal *law* in our house, the highest priority, to protect each other and to never embarrass or hurt another family member outside the house. The "co-author" of that family "law", my mother, had quite apparently, in a premeditated, careless, nonchalant manner, deliberately and maliciously betrayed me and betrayed our family trust. If I had had the means, I would probably have killed her.

That same summer, I remember being at the top of the stairs listening to my father talking to my mother in the living room calling her in a quiet, calm voice a fat slob and telling her to either stop drinking or get out. Then is when I learned that she was drinking. I was confused, hurt, and angry. I cried even though I hadn't cried in a very long time. I remember having no one to comfort me, all I could do was develop a way to "deal with it." I had only the strengths of a thirteen year old. I know now that I was on my way to becoming sick.

I believe today that the most painful part of my mother's drinking, probably also the most damaging, was the fact that my mother was never present for me emotionally. This does not anger me anymore now but it hurt me a lot then. My counselor tells me that her not being present is a big reason why I can't get close to women, why I don't trust people, women or men either for that matter. I'm working through those problems. My biggest one, the need to be liked, is in conflict with both of those. I need to be liked and I demand it of anyone who gets near me. I test them all the time and when they can't measure up to my satisfaction I cut them off. Most of the time they get tired of my games and cut me off. Like one woman told me, "You act like you want to punish every woman who gets near you and yourself too." "Sado-masochist," she called me. I'm working on it. I've discovered that if I can talk about my personal self, I can trust better. Sounds crazy. It should work the other way around. The more you can trust the more you should be able to reveal. Typical though with the child of an alcoholic or at least with me, everything works in reverse!

*I've always suspected that at some level older children recognize that being emotionally deprived is going to hurt them later on.*

The child of an alcoholic hurts a lot. The biggest hurt I live with is my sense of being different. That hurt takes away my confidence, always makes me feel very uncomfortable with people. Truly this hurt sometimes makes me want to cry and makes me want to drink. I need to be constantly aware and in touch with this hurt if I am to stay healthy. this is very difficult to do. Doing so is exhausting and frustrating and provides additional pain.

Right now I want to cry for I feel all the old pain all over again. Seems as if I brought it all back by writing this. I just don't know any words to fully convey the intensity of it all.

*The tears were a function of intense conflict between*

To continue with the incident, I remember standing at the top of the stairs listening to my father giving her the ultimatum and silently (but with tears streaming down my face) cheering him and applauding him with a never before felt intensity as if our team were making a *the pleasure* comeback and sticking it in the opponent's face. Yeah, *and guilt* Dad!!! Yeah!!! I was hating her at this time and feeling *he felt at* very guilty about that feeling but it was true and real *hearing* and could not be denied any longer, only felt and han- *his mother* dled with whatever worked. I was approximately four *demeaned.* months away from weekend drunks and a self taught crash course in constant drug abuse.

That summer was the summer of '73. That was really the beginning of me witnessing my mother's drinking. At least that is when I begin remembering her drinking. That Christmas was the last of her drinking that I remember. My mother stopped drinking follow- ing that Christmas.

Anyway, that Christmas was a chamber of horrors. I remember my mother either was drunk or angry the whole season. I remember her as fat, ugly, and yelling. I remember her rage tantrums and demeaning irra- tionalities. They seemed to permeate every square inch of me and of the house. I was becoming sick of it all and *I* was drinking and getting drunk whenever I could. God, I was angry with her. I wanted desperately to pro- tect my little sister who was five years old at the time from this unpredictable raging mad woman. This was becoming my main concern and the main concern of my older brother and older sister to protect the most vulnerable one.

That Christmas I wanted a guitar, a professional guitar. I had been taking guitar lessons for about three years and it was time to get a "real" guitar instead of trying to play a Sears. Christmas Eve our family was opening our gifts. I knew I was getting a guitar because no matter how hard one tries, it's awfully hard to wrap a guitar. My mother drunk, sweating, yelling said, "Here, Paul" and threw it at me. Suddenly I felt like punching her when what I really wanted was for her to be the beautiful mother I had at other Christmases. I couldn't believe her, I just couldn't believe her. At this time I seemed to be staring at the ground a lot, angry and silent. I acted that way that Christmas, afraid to look people in the eyes. It was that Christmas she stormed out of the house and stayed at a local motel. God, I was so unhappy that Christmas. I was only thirteen.

My mother's drinking ended that Christmas. She got sober and has been sober since. We have never been closer and my understanding of what happened is increasing every day. Most of the pain that I experienced has been revived by writing this. I'm glad. I'll always remember the incidents I have written here. It's what keeps me sober.

## Notations

The story which preceded and the one which follows speak of loneliness, hurt, and emotional deprivation. Both tell us that the worst aspects of being the children of an alcoholic lie not in any physical or corporal abuse but in the utter indifference in which the children are physically and emotionally steeped. Alcohol literally put up a wall between them and their respective parents, a wall which effectively blocked any affection or communication.

As children they understood nothing of the why for it and because they didn't, they came to assume that they were in some measure responsible for it. So they felt guilty. The guilt in turn compounded their bewilderment, their hurt, and their sense of aloneness.

This sense of aloneness is the key to understanding these two stories and indeed the stories of the vast preponderence of children of alcoholics. What they tell us is that when mom and/or dad are alcoholic no learning and no growth occur. What these stories more than imply is that children of alcoholics may well be stunted emotionally.

That these two people learned that suggests that other children of alcoholics have learned it too and/or are at least sensitive to the lack in their emotional development. In such an awareness lies much hope. For such an awareness can lead to a strong motivation to structure a more healthful environment for their children. In such an environment positive acceptance would be a given, love would be demonstrated, and a high value would be placed on truth.


# DAUGHTER OF ALCOHOLIC PARENTS
## (As Reported By The Daughter)


Fear, insecurity and illness are what fill my childhood memories. I was the only daughter in a family with two children. My brother is six years older than I.

Today I know better why my childhood was such a painful experience. It's one which I still feel I must deal with and which I know I will be dealing with all of my life. You see, the illness which fills my childhood memories was alcoholism.

My father's alcoholism was made apparent to me by his absence. He was always at the "corner." The "corner" was the Red Pheasant Bar. For some sick, sick reason I've always felt that I was the cause of my dad's drinking and absenteeism from home. Somewhere in my crazy thinking and feelings I concluded that he drank because I was bad. *A very common reaction among the children of alcoholics.*

My mother worked. She was around more but not much more. When she felt the need to explain why she wasn't home more which was almost never, she said it was her work. What I realize now is that it was her illness. Mother was alcoholic too.

I had a lot of baby sitters. All of them acted like they wished they were someplace else. They almost never talked to me. I guess that's why I don't remember a single one today.

When my mother *was* home she acted as if I was invisible. Sometimes when I asked a question she didn't answer. That might be because she was drunk. I'm not sure. It doesn't matter. It hurt me then just as much whether she was or not. It still hurts.

When my father did come home my mother's spaced out indifference vanished. She ranted and raged at him and he at her. On the very few occasions that I asked them please to stop they screamed at me, both of them at the same time. I remember being terrified, my stomach doing roll-overs. I remember deciding never again to ask them to stop.

*What she learned was that she was emotionally damned whether she did or did not try to interfere!*

My father's absenteeism and my mother's indifference made me feel like I was an albatross around their necks. What I'm trying to say is that as a little girl I was a walking bundle of guilt. I felt guilty because she had to have baby sitters for me. (She always complained about the expense.) I felt guilty if I spilled a glass of milk, even with the baby sitters. Come to think of it, I felt guilty for being alive.

At age four I became very ill with asthma. I always suspected that I got it because I was so desperate for attention. Suddenly my mother became very concerned and attentive. My asthma became worse. I remember one time telling her I was ill when I was feeling O.K. and in the process of telling her bringing on a severe asthmatic attack.

I never had an asthmatic attack with my father. Maybe it's because I knew instinctively that he would be repelled by it and would never even acknowledge my presence any more if I did.

My parents marriage ended when I was six years old. Then came the ultimate rejection. They put me and my brother in the custody of my aunt (my father's sister) and her husband.

Leaving my parent's house was emotionally wrenching. I didn't know that then. I know it now. I walked out with a pillow case stuffed with clothes. I don't remember who left with me, only that no one even held my hand. I remember feeling very nervous about my uncle, wondering if he was going to "do things" to me at his house.

In my aunt's house I became the "good little girl," perfect, always doing as I was told. I never spoke from any real feeling. At the same time I became their little clown. I did things, said things (even as a little girl I had a way with words) that would make them laugh. I learned quickly that clowns get a lot of attention. I became the best of all possible clowns.

My asthma disappeared in my aunt's house. She *And so* just never gave me attention for being sick. She also *fantasy* gave me more time than both my parents put together *became* and something they never gave me—gifts. As I said, for *an impor-* a long time I was scared of losing this second home. I *tant part* used to fall asleep at night imagining that I was *of her* Cinderella. Maybe I did things or acted like a Cinderella *life.* because I was given chores and responsibilities far beyond what was usually expected of people my age. At seven I washed, dried, and put away the supper dishes. At eight I did the food shopping at a local store with a shopping list made up mostly by me. At ten I was making supper. I was treated like an adult, really taken advantage of. I didn't care. That's how much I needed approval. Only recently did I realize that I never had a childhood. At the same time I was never encouraged to make decisions on my own nor made to stand responsible for the wrongs I did outside. Outside the house my aunt always got me out of trouble especially in school matters. I hated school. I hated homework, especially the discipline of doing it every night. My aunt and my uncle never made me do it, never told me to do it, never even asked about it. They could have cared less. When the teacher called or wrote, my aunt would go and talk to her and "fix it." So I learned to be irresponsible.

I was given many material and "nice" things in this *What she's* home but never was hugged or kissed or shown love. My *telling us* aunt and uncle were basically undemonstrative. I *here is that* overate. It was my love substitute. I became obese. Both *she was deprived the privilege of learning to find reward in loving.*

my obesity and my poor grades got me the attention I guess I needed so badly. I began to purchase my friends, giving them some of the gifts that I realize now my aunt gave me to buy her friendship.

Soon after I moved in my uncle coerced me into going down into the cellar, to his "hobby" shop he called it. There I became my uncle's new found hobby. I became a victim of sexual molestation.

In a woman's support group they told me that I don't get along with men because I want their attention too much. It's true. All my life I've wanted their attention. My therapist says that that "need" as she calls it started with my father. My uncle taught me that I'd get all kinds of attention if I was "nice" to him. What I learned early was that being "nice" to men also gave me some gratification.

*Her escape into alcoholism may have been due in part to the fact that her fantasy life was simply not rich or substantial enough to insulate her from the loneliness and isolation of her real life.*

I used what I had learned about sex as a child to get the attention I still craved during adolescence. I was "nice" to boys. I became popular. I also became alcoholic. I began drinking in junior high and drank my way through high school and beyond. I remember very little about my adolescence. It was lost in an alcoholic blur.

That same need for attention and the gratification I got from sex as a child and adolescent weren't very strong bases for developing a good relationship with a man. Even so when I was twenty-one I got married. If you haven't concluded it already let me tell you plain out, by twenty I was confused as I could possibly be about myself. My husband was much like me, scared, insecure, and alcoholic. When two dependent people marry it's a lot like the halt leading the blind. The marriage produced two children and lasted for thirteen miserable years. My eighteen year old son doesn't drink at all. My twenty year old daughter is a recovering alcoholic and attends A.A. with me.

The biggest problem I have today at age forty-two is a sense of insecurity. A therapist told me once it comes from my sense of rootlessness. That sense started with mom and dad who split up and then sent me away. It continued in my aunt's house where I wasn't permitted to be a child. Then it continued with a husband who was never much of a mate or provider.

But every cloud has a silver lining. My sense of rootlessness is probably the reason that I've become very active in the program of A.A. and Al Anon. Both give me a sense of purpose. Just as important for me, they give me a feeling of belonging to a large and very *She has channelized her energy and her love in a socially productive way.* stable organization.

# Part IV

# THE

# SINGLE

# PARENT

# FAMILY

# Chapter 8

# DYNAMICS AND EFFECTS

Single parent alcoholic families* suffer from all the problems of the two parent alcoholic alcoholic families discussed in Part I and they suffer from them more intensely. They do so for a simple and obvious reason. Single parents face the 'world alone. They have to deal alone with all those who impinge on the family—teachers, repairmen, doctors, creditors, and so forth. When the children are small, they have to take care of all of the mundane but necessary family chores by themselves: shopping, cooking, laundry, and so forth.

A constant and acute worry for many single parents, especially women with few vocational skills, is the lack of money. Because of this lack an important but very unpleasant part of their interpersonal scene is composed of social workers and/or lawyers; social workers because

---

*While occasionally a grandparent or other adult relative may be living in the single parent family, the focus here will be the more common one adult situation.

single parents often are or seek to be on welfare and lawyers because they need to obtain or maintain alimony payments. Many have to deal with both.

Small wonder that under circumstances such as these many single parents come to feel that life is a battle and a losing one at that. Alcoholic or not, many develop the classical alcoholic perception of a harsh threatening world filled with uncaring, unkind, if not hostile people. The possible responses to such a perception are many, vary, and sometimes blend. They are anger, bewilderment, withdrawal, and apathy. None are enhancing. All are conducive to a sense of victimization, a sense which they pass to one or more of their children. In a large measure because of this sense, parent and/or children turn to alcohol.

Single parents, male or female, even if healthy and alcohol free are hard pressed indeed to meet the basic psychological needs of their children. Excepting for the occasional death of a spouse, single parents are single and alone because of desertion, divorce, legal separation, or a refusal to cohabit. Whether any of these reasons were or were not of their choice, most single parents feel the guilt of having contributed to the failure, i.e., they contributed to the failure therefore *they* are failures. Self-condemnatory thinking like this, fairly common among single parents, is a prime reason so many suffer acutely from a low self-esteem for a long time into their single parent status. As was noted in Chapter 1, the ingredients of a positive self-esteem are security and love. Thus, the single parent who feels insecure and unloved is in something less than an ideal position to focus and meet those same needs in a child. When that parent looks to alcohol for help, the child's needs are never met.

The dynamic interchange between alcoholic and enabler varies from family to family but is especially insidious and destructive in the single parent family. The interchange is so because while the scenarios may vary with family the parent figure can be only alcoholic or an enabler. From the parent figure children derive their security, love, and self-esteem.

Now, the parent who is both single and alcoholic structures an environment which not only can not meet these needs but which indeed threatens and violates them. More often than not, children in these circumstances usually have suffered much even before the departure of their other parent. Not uncommonly, discord, conflict, and even battles preceded that departure. Even so any relief which children might obtain from the departure is quickly erased by the guilt they feel for feeling relieved, by the guilt feeling that they somehow precipitated the departure, by the guilt and selfishness felt when asking anything from a harried parent, and/or by the sudden strangeness of living with only one parent. This melange of feelings would prevent the child's security needs from being met even if the parent were able to do so.

Single alcoholic parents are hard put to communicate love to their children. A constant lack of time prevents them from parentally involving themselves in their children's lives or even from talking to them in a relaxed or playful way. (The exception to the last might occur in the glow of the first or second drink). *This lack of time together with their guilt, mundane but pressing household demands,* and *their own sense of emotional depreviation all combine to communicate to children that they are unloved.* This communication together with strong feelings of insecurity are the reasons these children acquire a poor self-esteem. This poor self-esteem stays with most of them throughout their lives and effects the problems listed and discussed in Part III.

A frequent and unfortunate response, usually by the senior child to an alcoholic single parent, is to assume the characteristics of the enabler. He/she becomes the person who brings order into a disorderly situation. The routine household tasks left undone by the alcohol dependent parent are taken over by the child. *As the parent's dependency on alcohol increases, the child begins to take on more and more responsibilities and in time assumes the role of parent abdicated by the alcoholic.* In some single parent families the situation becomes especially bizarre when the parent literally regresses into the role of just another child leaving the enabler child to parent everybody including him/herself. The only activity in which such a parent engages is buying the booze to maintain the role reversal.

The single parent family where the parent is alcoholic and has young children, while a fairly common situation, is of course not the only one. Single parents may have adolescent children. When they do, the possible effects are two and neither is desirable. Thus the adolescent may identify with the parent and become alcoholic or may react to the parent, become a teetotaler and an enabler too. As an enabler such a person takes on many of the dispositions and personality characteristics of the alcoholic parent but stays dry. Such a person is an excellent candidate to marry an alcoholic or to pass on the alcoholic disposition to the next generation.

# Chapter 9

# CASE REPORTS
# BY ALCOHOLIC
# SINGLE PARENTS

### Single Parent—Mother
**(As Reported By The Alcoholic Single Parent)**

I grew up in an alcoholic family. My father is alcoholic. I have a brother and sister who are alcoholic. I married an alcoholic and I am myself an alcoholic who's been sober for five years. Alcohol was and is the major reason why my life is as it is.

Today I am parenting three children alone. Their ages 4, 6, and 9. The middle one, sandwiched between two girls, is a boy. I've been divorced for a little over three years and when I think about it and I do a lot, I think that when I die I can go only one way, up because my life on earth has been an anxious hell for so long.

I love my children. I know that in my bones. I love them so much that I chose to get a divorce. I love them so much that I had to get them out of the craziness of living in the same house with an alcoholic. Alcohol turns people inside out. It makes kind people cruel and gentle people violent. It did that to my father. I grew up scared of him. I didn't want that for my kids. So I sued for divorce.

Alcohol perverts people sexually. I know because growing up in my father's house I was sexually abused from the time I was eight until I was twelve and always by the same person, my brother who was ten years older. That same brother raped me right after I was divorced. When I told my parents, they both asked me what I had done to "make him do such a thing." When I had him arrested my father got very angry with me and yelled a lot. My father has been dry for ten years but it's only recently that he's beginning to change. My mother refused to talk to me for a long time because my father reported, "I had stuck a dagger in her heart." My mother doesn't drink, never has, but living with my father for almost forty years has made her alcoholic. She thinks like one, talks like one, and acts like one. I didn't want to grow up to be like my mother. So I sued for divorce.

My sister is alcoholic and she's been married to one for thirteen years. They have two children. Her husband abuses all three of them. He beats them sometimes when he's drunk and she puts up with it. She's so scared of him that over the years she's become a submissive jellyfish. She's confided to me that he cheats on her. He even brags about it to her. She puts up with it, continues to sleep with him. That's how scared she is to be on her own. That's how dependent she's become. My brother and my ex-husband are very good friends. They talk about women the same way. I guess I knew instinctively

As I read this I think it is a marvel that this woman has not lost contact with reality! I think too that being reared in an alcoholic home gives one the impression that the whole world is so! Or at least that madness is part of life.

that in time my husband would cheat on me. So I sued for divorce.

I wrote before that I love my children so much that I got a divorce. That divorce was the turning point of my life. I still marvel at the fact that I did it. I came from a family where traditionally the men treated the women like dirt and the women felt they should be. I broke with that tradition. With my divorce (the first in the family) I broke with a lot of traditions. I amazed me and my family even more when I started college. "How can you do this thing when you've got three kids." My father yelled that at me at least once a week during my whole first year of college. I'm going to graduate next May but it hasn't been easy. It's been hell. I've wondered often why I've been willing to put up with so much and I decided it was because for the first time in my life I am living the way I *choose* to live. I wasn't living in the hell created by my husband, or my father, or anybody else. If it's hell, at least it's my own. There's . another reason too. Hope. Going to college gives me hope for my future. I've gotten through a lot of very bad days because I know that the future will be better. Going to college gives me something else. Every day in a lot of ways I learned what I always suspected about me. I'm smart. Nobody ever told me that until I got to college.

*This is a woman with incredible energy and determination.*

What's it like being the single parent of three little kids? It's very hard. How do I manage? I'm not sure. I'm busy every single minute of every day and evening and I sleep no more than five or six hours a night. My day begins at 5:30 so I can get my shower in before Martha and the kids need the toilet. Martha is a fifteen year old who lives with us. She's an alcoholic who I volunteered to take in. The Department of Mental Health for the state pays me to do that. God knows we can use the money because we're on welfare. I didn't do it only for that reason though. I did it mostly because I felt I can help her stay sober. I'm majoring in psychology. I want to work as a probation officer or counselor of some kind. I see living with her as good experience for me. Besides that, Martha's a help with the kids.

*I wonder if there isn't more resentment in her toward them than she admits to?*

The kids, they're my life. They're the reason my life's been so hard since the divorce. They also give my life a lot of meaning today. It's hard imagining what my life would be without them. I know it would be easier. There'd be so many fewer worries. It would be less hectic and if nothing else, I could take my shower later! But their mine and helping them become the best people they can be is a goal which makes my life worth living.

I worry about them all the time, Mathew especially. Jan who's four and Linda who's nine seem to get along pretty well. Linda already has a lot of friends and does well in school. Jan is in a day care when I'm in college and seems to love it. Mathew who is only six is the one I'm concerned about. He still soils himself occasionally during the day and wets the bed regularly. I know these problems will disappear in time but I wonder often what their residue will mean for him later. Unlike a lot of women I believe a lot of Freud. "Our earliest learnings stay with us longest." He said something like that.

I shudder when I think of what poor Mathew went through during his first couple of years of life. Both his father and I were alcoholic and drunk during most of the time. I feel guilty about that and I can't walk away from it like his father has done. I live with it every day and what's worse is that something is always happening to remind me that he's not as healthy as he should be. The kindergarten teacher used to call me several times a month about how he was fighting with kids or pouting or soiling his pants. It was always something. Last week I got a call from his first grade teacher. She's had to seat him next to her desk because "his concentration isn't what it should be" but she said, "He's great one on one." I know what all that means. He's starved for attention. Sometimes the guilt becomes so intense I want to rant and rage and scream and I can't. I want to scream why me, God? I don't. I don't because no one

*This woman is in counseling.*

would really care. If they did, what could they do? Enough about Mathew and me and my guilt.

My biggest personal, emotional concern, might be him but there are others. The biggest practical concern is money. Like Mathew it's on my mind always. It doesn't make me feel guilty like Mathew does but it keeps me anxious and worried and it does so all the time. I've tried but I can't even imagine what life would be like not having to be concerned about money.

The reality is I'm poor. Very poor, and I'm on welfare. If you don't know, let me tell you, welfare recipients are treated like they're less than human. I don't know why but the system has it set up so that it's the banks who disburse the food stamps. They shouldn't because the only people bank people treat with respect are people with money. The rest they treat like scum. The hours that I can pick up my stamps for the month are very limited, two to four Thursday and Friday. If I miss, it's tough luck. I've been told the stamps are in the big safe and it can't be opened except at those hours. When the clerk counts them out to me, she counts them and hands them to me like they were coming out of her pocket. I always feel ashamed picking them up. I've been told I shouldn't. I do though. I feel ashamed spending them. I hear the whispers and impatient sighs behind me. Once I heard the comment, "Why the Christ doesn't she go to work?"

Anyway, we never have enough money, even for food. The two days before the welfare check arrives are the worse, no matter how well I plan. Those are our oatmeal days. In August and September I can supplement that with fresh vegetables from the garden.

Clothes are a real problem with three little kids. Linda seems to outgrow her clothes every week. I've learned to buy in thrift shops. Everything I buy is out of style for us, but I have no alternative.

The only good deal I have is my apartment. It's lovely. It's in a nice section and it's subsidized housing.

There's just no cash even for anything. God forbid my car breaks down. The last time it did, my father paid the repair bill. I hated to ask him but I didn't see what else I could do. I did and he came through. In his own way he has some feelings for me and my kids. He's helped me other times in a pinch. I know he has because he feels guilty for his years of drink. I don't like to do so but I use his guilt. When you're a single parent you do what you have to!

How am I able to go to college? Loans. I'll be paying back these loans for about seven or eight years after I graduate.

My day ends late and when I crawl into bed I'm tired and I usually go off to sleep as quickly as one of my babies. Sometimes I don't though. Sometimes I lie awake for a while and I know why. I'm lonely. Despite my hectic schedule and the pressures of my kids and money and school, I'm lonely. I have no time for me. I'm still young and pretty and I see men still look at me. My problem is I can't afford to look back at them. I just don't have the time or the energy. When I weaken and let myself realize that, then I really get lonely.

## Notations

What the preceding and following story tell us is that those who would be single parents will be able to cope more effectively in that role if they cultivate the qualities of fortitude, energy, courage, and hope. Single parents, we learn, need an infinite amount of patience and if they want better for themselves and their children, they must be in constant motion—going, doing, and accomplishing. All the while these parents, male or female, must take on, learn, and persevere in tasks and roles that are new and thereby often anxiety-provoking.

In addition, single parents need to learn to cope with the insidious stress of loneliness. This is especially true when the children are little as in the preceding story. but it is true in general too, because they are not living with mates with whom they can share the anxieties and the incidental joys of child rear-ing. Any ventilation and sharing must await the scheduled time of support groups and/or the counselor.

The virtue of hope is a powerful emotional support for single parents. The search for an ultimately better life makes all the pain, loneliness, and anxiety of their role, if not acceptable, at least tolerable. Still these parents worry. For they know that while they rear their children in a setting free of alcohol they know, and painfully well, that the psychological effects of alcohol are very real, very insidious, and very enduring. However, as they cope with those effects they show their children that one can indeed deal with alcoholism. And herein lies their hope. For they know that this very coping provides their children (them too) with the emotional wherewithal to live happier and more successful lives.

## SINGLE PARENT—FATHER

### (As Reported By The Father)

I'm not alcoholic but alcohol made me the single parent of a sixteen year old girl and a fourteen year old boy. Six months ago I told my wife to either stop drinking or get out. She got out. My wife of almost two decades had come to love alcohol more than she loved her family.

I'm a personnel manager for a major computer corporation. Communication is my business. I've been told that I'm articulate and that I'm a good listener. My job evaluations always rate me the highest in "approachability" and "likeableness." Simply put, people see me as a decent guy. The reason is simple. I respect people. I always have. I respected my wife as much as I loved her. In the end the best I could feel for her was indifference.

*True. Alcoholism destroys love.*

Elaine and I met in our senior year in college. We married the following year. She said that all that she wanted was to be a wife and mother. I believed her. I had no reason not to. When feminism took hold she never seemed to take to it. She might have been sympathetic toward it but she never got passionate about it either.

Her prime concerns were about her home, her kids, and me. She was an excellent housewife, neater even than the proverbial pin. I never remember dust or dirt in my house, on my clothes, or on my kids during the first fifteen years or so of our marriage.

*an illustration of how low self-esteem can not tolerate criticism.* I didn't think anything about her cleanliness until a friend of ours who was working on her master's degree in psychology kidded her that her scrupulous concern with cleanliness reflected strong feeling of guilt. I can still remember Elaine's response. Pure fury. I remember it not only because of the intensity of it but because she made a scene at the party where we were. This was the first time I'd seen her mad. I didn't realize it then but it was also the first time I'd seen her criticized.

On the surface she seemed to be a far better mother than most. She did all the usual things mother did. She fixed breakfast for the kids every morning, got them off to school, and was always there with cookies and milk when they got home.

When my daughter, Jean, was in the first grade, Elaine decided that she and my son, Paul, should know the classics. She or I had to read to them every night whether they wanted to be read to or not. That got to be boring for them even painful and ended only after I joined the kids in the protest.

Somewhere in the middle of the classics ordeal, she decided the kids should know "good music." She went out and bought a lot of operatic and symphonic records. So literally for months they would go off to sleep to Italian arias and concertos that I'm sure the kids learned to hate. If they complained, she yelled. If I tried to step in, she'd turn on me screaming that I was turning them against her. Some of the scenes were pretty bad, so bad I remember them only vaguely.

Next she found records that taught and identified bird calls. For weeks we all woke up to birds chirping and a soft, cooing female voice telling us what we were hearing. No one complained, probably because no one wanted to hear mommy yell.

Elaine liked to see herself as a gourmet cook. We'd have two or three dinner parties a month. She cooked French, Italian, and Oriental. Sometimes her dishes came out fine. Often they did not. When they didn't, she blamed me or the kids. Over the years that had become her explanation for her failures. She never could admit when something was her fault or when she was wrong. I got so used to her henpecking me that I never even noticed when there was just the family around. I probably shouldn't have let that happen because she began to do it in front of guests. I only noticed that because I could see people look away embarrassedly. After the company would leave, we began to have some awful fights. These fights became a regular affair. Once, probably because I'd had too much to drink, I called her on her henpecking at the table. She glared at me and picked on me throughout the meal. The guests that night left right after dessert and never accepted another invitation.

*Another symptom of a low self-esteem.*

People had such a lousy time at our house that few of them reciprocated. Her reputation as a hostess and as a person to be with must have spread because we were almost never invited anywhere. That bothered Elaine a lot. A couple of times I tried to explain to her why it might be. On those occasions she just ranted and raged and refused to accept my explanation even when I said that I was to blame too because I would fight with her in front of people. She refused to accept any notion that she was at all responsible. She became embittered and stopped inviting people to our house. We became social isolates.

My best guess now is that she started drinking about the time we stopped having people in. She began to act differently. Never one to be especially interested

*Her sudden excessive interest in sex was probably a response to her self-doubt with her sense of femininity.*

*I'd bet her alcoholic-like drinking began before this first reported knowledge of it.*

*mixed messages typical of alcoholic.*

in sex, she suddenly began to want it every night and sometimes more than once in the course of the night. Where she had always been rather boring and prudish on how we were to do it, she suddenly developed an acute interest in various erotic techniques and methods. She developed an insatiable appetite for oral sex, to perform it and to have it performed on her. At first I was delighted but then as her demands increased, I began to protest, initially in a joking way. Then one night when I awoke for the third time to her ministrations, I protested that I was too tired. She went beserk. She screamed that I didn't love her, that I was seeing another woman, and that I was inadequate sexually. What bothered me most about that scene was that I know that the kids had heard her, if not the neighbors too. She left the bedroom and slept on the living room couch for the rest of the night. I didn't dare go after her for fear of another scene. The next morning I found her asleep still naked, a half empty quart of Gilbey gin on the coffee table beside her. I covered her up and that morning for the first time I got the kids their breakfast.

When I came home from work I found her quiet, contrite, and apparently anxious to make amends. We had sex that night but her participation was only dutiful, mechanical. That way she let me know that her heart wasn't in it. From about that point on, the only consistent thing about Elaine were her mixed messages.

Family life began to deteriorate. I realize now that the deterioration was tied to her drinking. Her compulsive housewifely neatness and sense of order evaporated slowly but nevertheless evaporated. Dust began to accumulate. The washing began to pile up. The kids and I began to wear clothes that were unironed. Where formerly I found supper on the table, I would arrive home at my usual time and find her preparing it, all the while complaining loudly how she got no help and no gratitude for her efforts.

We all tried to help. Jean began to get the supper, I began to do the washing, and Paul the housecleaning. I think the kids did because they wanted to please her. I did because I wanted peace. However, no matter what *and so they all became unwitting enablers!* our motives nor how hard we tried our lives were something less than peaceful. On those evenings when Jean got supper and those evenings became more and more frequent, Elaine was impossible. She complained loudly that the food was overcooked or undercooked. More than once she complained that it was both! More than once Jean left the table crying. Elaine would jump up and literally drag her back and make her eat. In these first episodes I tried to play a soothing peacemaker and usually only succeeded in making things worse as Elaine would complain loudly that I never supported her. I didn't, she would say, because I basically didn't love her, never had loved her. All I wanted, she would scream at the tenth decibel, was to turn the kids against her. Paul, who had always been a quiet kid especially at the dinner table, became positively mute-like.

What amazes me about it all now is that I didn't *I think she needed professional help—* realize what was happening to Elaine, to us. Even as I began to do more and more, like the food shopping for example, I still didn't see what was happening. I attributed her vitrolic diatribes at supper to being crabby. She'd always been like that I told myself. Of course *Indeed family therapy would have been eminently appropriate.* she'd resent Jean's cooking, she couldn't stand competing with anyone. In this shoddy thinking process, I conveniently refused to see that Elaine needed help. I wonder now, had she received it then, would it all have turned out as it did? In any case I didn't see any significant problem. I refused to see things as they were. I wanted peace.

Then I found my first bottle. I was doing the vacuuming that Paul did ordinarily when I rolled a bottle out from under the couch with the vacuum wand. Gin. I didn't think anything about it! I remember putting it on the coffee table as I vacuumed and later putting it in the trash. That's how much I wanted peace!

Elaine's sexual advances ended. If I turned to her after we'd gone without it for a couple of weeks or so, she would respond unpredicatably. Sometimes she was incredibly responsive and passionate but sometimes she rejected me with a long, loud, abusive stream of verbal vulgarities. I stopped turning to her, a little because she began to disgust me, a little because I was actually learning to fear her, and a lot because I didn't want my kids to know about our sex life.

She began to have trouble sleeping. She would get up in the middle of the night and stay up for a couple of hours. Sometimes I'd find her passed out on the living room couch in the morning. Even though the kids and I would talk and make a lot of noise on purpose, we could hear her drunken snores while we ate breakfast.

Her appearance began to deteriorate. She who had been personally neat to the point of being fastidious began to look like a slob. Her blouses, her skirts, her bathrobes were stained more often than not. Her eyes were usually bleary and red and her hair was always unfashionably long and sometimes unkempt.

Things began to come to a head when she had a bad auto accident. The city police called me at work just as I was leaving to go home. They asked me to come pick her up at the station. I found her sleeping in the waiting room, sprawled out on a bench, hair awry, her blouse sticking out of her skirt, a stomach pot disgustingly evident. Her head was slumped back, spittle was oozing out of the corner of her mouth. I felt embarrassed, sorry for her, for me too and I was angry. Angrier than I'd ever been in my life.

I didn't wake her but saw the police sergeant who told me that she had totaled the car when she had gone off the road. No one else had been involved. The sergeant looked at me sympathetically. "You got a problem there, Mister." Then he added not unkindly, "She was lucky." Actually she was very unlucky. Unfortunately for her and me, her husband, drunken driving was not yet viewed as the cardinal sin which it is today. Today she would have had to appear in court, probably been fined, would have lost her license for sure, and perhaps been given a suspended sentence. She certainly would have had to attend a workshop for "Driving Under the Influence." Instead she underwent no punishment. She just walked out of the police station with me groggily, grumpily, and with no remorse.

I remember the conversation we had driving home. "Please stop at the Colonial," she said. "I want to get a bottle of something."

"No more bottles Elaine."

"What do you mean no more bottles?" Her tone was sharp, belligerent.

I replied firmly. "Just that. No more bottles. You're going to have to stop drinking. You're alcoholic."

She screamed her response. "Stop this fucking *Classically* car!" In the past six months maybe longer she had taken *alcoholic* to vulgarities whenever she'd felt frustrated. For Elaine, *reaction!* to be contradicted was to be frustrated. I paid no need to her rantings and drove home.

For once I was angrier and more resolved than she. When we arrived home she jumped out, ran to our bedroom and locked herself in. I called Alcoholics Anonymous and asked for help. They sent over a man and woman. Elaine refused to come out and speak to them or to me either. I lay on the couch that night tossing and turning. Periodically I wept.

The next morning I called in sick to work. I got the kids off to school and waited by the bedroom door for her to come out. When she finally did, I glanced at her embarrassedly. She glared in return and looked, I decided, far less weary than I felt. We talked, more accurately I talked and told her about what the people from A.A. had told me that she needed help but had to ask for it. I gave her their number and promised her all the help and support she would ever need. I also told her I loved her and wanted our marriage to continue. She listened and cried a little. I was heartened by that. It was the first contrition she'd shown yet. I made her breakfast and we drank coffee and talked. She called A.A. and got a schedule of the meetings.

Altogether I felt it had been profitable morning. By noon I felt so good I took her out to lunch. Afterwards we cleaned the house together and like a pentitent little girl she brought out three empty quarts of gin from the bedroom. then she made supper. It was like a metamorphosis. She met the kids at the door when they got off the school bus. For the first time in months I felt that normality had come back into my house. When a woman from A.A. came by to take her to a meeting I was sure of it.

The climax came a week later when I got home and found her savagely beating up Jean with an old leather belt of mine. The whole scene was a nightmare. I wrestled her to the ground, forcibly brought her to the bedroom, and slammed the door. She locked herself in. I realized that she had liquor stashed in there. I didn't care. I had made up my mind to make the ultimate confrontation.

Again the next morning I waited outside her door. When she opened the door, she smelled of gin but she was rational. I felt like I was living some kind of soap opera as I told her I would pay any price that a treatment center would charge for her rehabilitation. I also reiterated that I would give her all the psychological support she wanted to stop drinking. But she had to stop. If she didn't, she had to get out. I felt nervous saying it but my voice was hard doing it. Her reaction surprised me. She never even answered. She just sighed, turned back into her bedroom, packed a medium sized suitcase, and left by cab.

My first feeling was one of relief. It still is. I didn't realize just how much tension and anxiety we had lived with until she left. When I told the kids that she had left, Paul just shrugged. Jean's words were, "That's too bad." But her tone was pure facetiousness.

We haven't seen her since the day she left. She's called us on the kids' birthdays and at Christmas (she missed last Christmas). We exchange "how you doings?" But they're not really sincere. What I found revealing about these phone chats is that the kids don't ask her to come back nor do I. We just don't miss her. Maybe it's because the pain is still too recent. Maybe we will in time. Meanwhile what a difference it is to come home to a home without an alcoholic! Supper, that we all take turns making, is a happy time. Occasionally we talk about her absence. I think we do, so that we can at least share the guilt we all live with. One of the first times we did Jean said, "She had to leave, daddy. If she continued drinking and stayed she would have destroyed all of us." I've thought a lot about that line of Jeans'. I doubt that alcoholism can destroy all families but I'm sure of this. No family can live with alcoholism and prosper.

*my conviction is that these three can profit from family counseling so that they can all come to truly believe Jean's words.*

# Part V

# DO'S

# AND

# DON'TS

**For Non-drinking Family Members**

# Chapter 10

# THE DO'S

To help the alcoholic member or members the non-drinking members of the family will more easily be able to do so if they

1. strengthen their own selves,

2. seek help,

3. strive constantly to enhance the alcoholic member,

4. establish a loving relationship with the alcoholic member, and

5. learn to relax about the problem.

# STRENGTHEN YOURSELF

A basic message of this book is that alcoholics emmotionally infect non-drinking members of the families. The members' best antidote for such infection is to *strengthen themselves.*

## Do Perceive The Alcoholic As A Person, A Worthy Person

The knowledge provided in this book about the disease and about the dynamics of alcoholic interaction should prove helpful in doing this. More helpful still would be for the non-drinking members to develop a system of thinking so that they can **perceive the alcoholics for the persons they are** rather than to focus and react to their sickness and to their sick ways.

As non-drinking members practice and learn this system of thinking they inevitably develop a clearer and more enhancing perception of themselves. With such a perception family members can come to perceive and interact with the alcoholic in a more healthful way for themselves as individuals, the alcoholic, and the family as an unit.

For the system of thinking that will strengthen yourself, the following activities will be helpful.

## Do Make Decisions Out Of Choice, Not Guilt

As noted in other contexts, guilt is ever present in the alcoholic family. It intrudes not only in decision making but, indeed, in most interactions. Members who learn not to let guilt dominate their thinking or their familial interactions will serve as a healthy example not only for children but for the alcoholic and any others disposed toward "guilty" thinking. Before making decisions, seek out the alternatives, examine the pros and cons of each, and decide on the bases of what is best. Make decision making become a conscious intellectual process, rather than an emotional process or one which finds its roots in guilt.

## Do Be Flexible

Recognize that absolutes have no place in intra-familial relations; no one member is "bad", not yourself and not the alcoholic either. To emotionally appreciate that a hard nosed, "black and white view" of self, of the alcoholic, or of any other member of the family will only block a fair and "total person" view. Certainly one must have "backbone" enough to make decisions but having done so recognize that other view points and perhaps additional information may need to be considered. Then when you do you may need to change the position (decision) you have made. Doing so may help others to recognize that new information is always welcomed and may indeed warrant reconsideration. Such behavior presents flexibility with justification.

## Do Maintain An Open Mind And Anticipate Discussion And Interactions

Naively optimistic expectations about yourself or the alcoholic are just as inappropriate as are pessimistic ones. The former put both under needless unrealistic pressure. The latter provide alcoholics with justification to persevere in their destructive behavior. The best way to maintain an open mind is to focus on actual behavior and to respond to it firmly but without exaggeration.

## Do Discriminate And Differentiate

See no person as his/her behavior, not yourself nor the alcoholic either. Such a perceptual stance will cause destructive thought patterns. If you think of a person as being the same as his/her behavior, then you are omitting a lot about that person that could be very meaningful to you. Accept another person as a total being of which behavior is only part. If you think of a person as being the same as his/her behavior, then you believe that an error will make him/her a failure. Then you soon will believe that a lapse by the alcoholic will occur and that sobriety will never be achieved. Then other family members will "catch" your belief, your attitude, and the alcoholic will not have the environmental support so essential to recovery. Learn to discriminate and differentiate among the many aspects of a person and accept his/her behavior as only one of those aspects.

## Do Share Your Feelings of Satisfaction

**Bask in those intrafamilial activities and interactions which give you a sense of enhancement.** If you as a non-drinking member feel good after a talk or outing with the alcoholic, the probability is strong that the alcoholic profited also. When you do feel good capitalize, rather than minimize it. Accept those positive feelings and especially share those feelings with the alcoholic. To reflect and communicate your feelings of satisfaction about intrafamilial activities to other family members is eminently appropriate and desirable.

## SEEK HELP

Non-drinking members can and should **seek help.** Just as the alcoholic must admit the need for help before he/she can get better, so must the non-drinking members admit and seek help. Much help is available. Two illustrations of organizations which have proved of benefit to many millions of people are Alcoholics Anonymous and Al-Anon Family Groups.

Both organizations operate on the premise that help for the alcoholic can be achieved only if family members learn the facts about the disease and integrate them into their own lives. This integration involves taking stock of their attitudes and values especially regarding alcohol and the diseased family member. Attendance at A.A. meetings and Al-Anon support groups facilitates this process of personal self-exploration. This is achieved because both organizations direct individuals to focus on their emotional involvement.

Individual counseling is probably the best way to come to understand the nature of one's emotional involvement. In the sheltered emotional climate provided by the counseling session the individual is free to explore his/her values, motives, and dynamics both as they affect him/her alone and in relation to the alcoholic. Also in the counseling process the individual can find support for the anxiety lived with at home and can vent frustrations, anger, and despair. In sum, individual counseling is a valuable resource and one which members of the alcoholic family should explore.

## STRIVE TO ENHANCE THE ALCOHOLIC

You and other non-drinking members of the alcoholic family should **strive constantly to enhance** the alcoholic in all ways possible. If you are to have any positive effect at all, these ways must be sincere, appropriate, and realistic. To be of assistance to the alcoholic you must compliment, express affection, and act out kindnesses from a heartfelt motive. If you don't, the alcoholic will most assuredly perceive it. Remember that a common alcoholic characteristic is an exquisite sensitivity to motive and a constant latent mistrust of another's motives. These attitudes prevail even toward family members. Accordingly, you and other family members who seek to enhance should be careful that any intentions to enhance are rooted in sincerity.

Any specific acts of enhancement, compliments, gifts, or expressions of love should be commensurate with the alcoholic's behavior. Like sincerity, excesses will be only suspect. You need especially to be aware when the alcoholic is motivated by guilt. Overly generous words, gifts, or acts are simply not appropriate for the alcoholic who is guiltily trying to compensate for inappropriate behavior. If you or other family members show or express such behaviors, you give the alcoholic a false message about the value and merit of what he/she does. Alcoholics do not need such a message as their perception of others' behavior and their own is distorted enough.

## Do Engage In Honest Talk

Talk can be a powerful instrument for good or ill. Talk makes people sick but it can make people well too. What researchers have discovered is that psychotherapeutic counseling has developed into an art because of the curative effects of talk. These curative effects are the reasons that mental health organizations, A.A., and Al-Anon base their therapeutic activities upon it.

In light of these discoveries, you and other non-drinking members of the alcoholic family would be well advised to strive for opportunities to **engage in honest talk** with the alcoholic as frequently as possible. The honest talk activity militates best against all the insidious and debilitating aspects of alcoholism.

When you get alcoholics to talk, you help them block their tendency to distance and isolate themselves. Both these tendencies engender the paranoia which in turn can lead to hostile and even brutal behavior intra-familially.

By you and the alcoholic engaging in honest talk (at least on your part), you can, if nothing else, help the alcoholic to become uncomfortable in his/her tendency to deny and thereby to distort the reality of the situation. For example, by talking alcoholics can be made to understand that family members do not accept the "I didn't drink that much" rationalization as an explanation for spending the previous evening inebriated in front of the television.

### Do Establish A Loving Relationship

The most important help that you and other non-drinking family members can provide is to **establish a loving relationship** with the alcoholic(s). Many alcoholics have become alcoholic precisely because they were never exposed to, or for some reason never profited from, a loving relationship. If you and if you can help other family members to bear these thoughts in mind and channel your energies in developing such a relationship with the alcoholic, you and the other family members can militate against the alcoholic's need to drink and better still, you can abet any signs of budding health.

### Do Show Acceptance And A Positive Regard

A loving relationship is one where respect is, one where no conditions are placed on acceptance and positive regard of the person. Therefore, to establish a loving relationship **show acceptance and positive regard for the alcoholic** and other family members. Alcoholics, whether they be adolescents or adults, usually have been reared and steeped in milieus which were exactly the opposite. Respect as a person was a virtual unknown for most of them and, if any acceptance did exist, it was always premised on conditions of performance.

### Do Provide A Sense Of Being A Peer

What alcoholics need most and what you can give in a loving relationship is **to provide a sense of being a peer.** They don't need parental, protective-like love or that of a big brother or big sister type. They need to experience the feelings of respect which come from being an equal. Only in such a relationship will they be able to acquire the self-respect so vital to healthful functioning. This self-respect is precisely what eludes most alcoholics and what promotes and aggravates their need to drink.

# LEARN TO RELAX

You and other members of the alcoholic family need to **learn to relax about the problem** of drink. You need to understand and emotionally appreciate that finally the problem is not yours but is indeed the alcoholic's.

### Do Help The Alcoholic With The Problem

**You can help the alcoholic with the problem**—*first,* by you and the alcoholic recognizing the situation as a problem; *second,* as a problem which can be overcome; and *third,* as yourself being a person who is able and willing to offer the support and other help so essential for the alcoholic to overcome the drinking.

### Do Turn Loose

**You need to relax, to turn loose, to recognize that you can not assume the problem for the alcoholic.** If you consciously or unconsciously try to take over the problem, to cure it, or eradicate it via intimidation, threats, anger, or sermons, you can and most often will make it worse. The problem and the responsibility for its alleviation belongs to the alcoholic. You and other family members need to remind yourselves of these simple facts again and again. An acceptance of them will help abate the frantic, compulsive-like behavior in which so many engage in order to assuage the guilt with which they must contend. Such behavior only increases anxiety in the alcoholic family.

### Do Let The Alcoholic Have The Responsibility

A simple truth but one which escapes the harried non-drinking family members is that **no one ever made anyone alcoholic.** Just as important to bear in mind is that **no adult is responsible for another normal adult's behavior, not legally, not morally, and especially not emotionally. To assume such a responsibility is to assume the role of enabler.**

### Do Control Your Time And Energy

The best way for you to relax about the problem is not to obsess about it but to **control the amount of time and energy devoted to it;** to rest and put it out of mind periodically; in short, to **compartmentalize it.** What this means is that you learn, and as much as possible help other non-drinking family members learn, to not let the alcoholic's addiction and the problems associated with it intrude on familial activities and relationships with the other family members. Activities of any and all kinds in which the alcoholic is invited are an excellent way to facilitate compartmentalization, i.e., outings, playing cards and games, doing household chores, and so forth. Note that the first five points outlined in this chapter are all directed toward this very end of compartmentalization.

# Chapter 11

# THE DON'TS

You and other non-drinking family members should know that certain behaviors by each of you facilitate and accelerate the progress of alcoholism. These behaviors are easier to understand when explained as do nots. The number of these behaviors are many but they all fall under one of the following two:

1. do not engage in alcoholic behaviors, and

2. do not enable.

## DO NOT ENGAGE IN ALCOHOLIC BEHAVIORS

You and other non-drinking members of the alcoholic family who seek to enhance **do not engage in alcoholic behaviors.** To prevent any such occurrence you must be sensitive to the dynamics* of the alcoholic.

---

*As noted in Chapter 1 these include perception, needs, and defenses.

### Don't Withdraw

If you are aware and appropriately responsible to the alcoholic's destructive dynamics, you will not feed them and you will **not withdraw** from them either. Withdrawal by you and/or other family members is invariably interpreted as indifference by the alcoholic and indifference confirms the alcoholic's notion that he/she is unloved and a victim. The stance you need to take and need to communicate is "I am here, to talk and help in any way that I can."

### Don't Procrastinate

Your help can best be given by behaving in ways which are directly opposite to those of the alcoholic. Thus, fulfill all your promises and **do not procrastinate** in any familial obligations.

### Don't Be Secretive

Do **not be secretive** in intrafamilial behaviors and especially in relation to the alcoholic. (There is no better way to engender paranoia!) Talk with other family members and with the alcoholic. In your talk be plain, open, and straightforward.

### Don't Be Indecisive

**Do not be indecisive** and **do not give double messages.** Such ways of relating can only compound the confusion which typically characterizes the system of communication in the alcoholic family.

### Don't Be Arbitrary

This system can be further ameliorated if you and other family members are flexible and open-minded. Thus **do not be arbitrary.**

### Don't Behave Impulsively

**Do not behave impulsively** and help other family members to not either. Rather, plan and demonstrate that mode as characterizing your behavior. Indeed, such planning should become central to all family activity. Meals and outings should be planned and whenever possible should involve and include the alcoholic. Excepting for familial emergencies, plans made should ordinarily be fulfilled.

### Don't Give Undue Attention

As a non-drinking members **do not give undue attention to the aches, pains, and minor illnesses** of the alcoholic or of any other family member for that matter. As noted, illness can play an important role in the alcoholic family's way of life. It can become a major factor in the family's interactions. Those especially prone toward illness seem to be the children who feel emotionally deprived. If given attention only when sick, they gravitate toward illness and learn to become hypochondrical.

### Don't Argue

Family members who seek to ameliorate the brooding, depressive, or emotionally charged climate of the alcoholic family **do not argue** with the alcoholic or with other family members. Arguments in such climates can and do lead to physical abuse and later recriminations and guilt.

Such arguments precipitate the alcoholic's drinking. If they were the abuser, they drink out of guilt. If they were bested in the argument or if they were the abused, they drink to comfort themselves. In either case they are provided with the rationalization to drink.

## DO NOT ENABLE

My experience in counseling alcoholic families is that when enablers are told what it means to enable they become angry. Their anger, I have learned, is a function of their genuine disbelief, their horror, or their simple embarrassment. Very simply, most people **do not** want to **enable.** Then why do they? The specific reasons are probably as numerous as there are enablers. However, underlying them all are three basic ones:

> the alcoholic's remarkable ability to manipulate,

> the enabler's misguided sense of love, and

> the enabler's terror of ultimately being left alone.

### Don't Overprotect

Many alcoholics are manipulators supreme. They sense the potential enablers' penchant for overprotection and instantly exhibit an acute need for love and attention. If you and other family members love healthfully, you **do not overprotect the alcoholic.** (See Chapter 2.)

## Don't Take Over Chores

Alcoholics spot the enablers' need for orderliness and neatness and they become positively cavalier about not picking up after themselves. If you and other family members want the alcoholic to be a contributing family member, then you **do not pick up after the alcoholic nor take over his/her chores.**

## Don't Assume Their Worries

Alcoholics quickly discern the enabler's tendency to shoulder familial worries and anxieties. Then the alcoholic lets the enabler do so. If the enabler seems temporarily free of worries, the alcoholic seems to deliberately generate new ones for the enabler. For these reasons you and other members will best be served and so will the alcoholic if you **do not assume the alcoholic's worries, do not solve the alcoholic's problems.**

## Don't Accept Their Promises

Trust between people is built and reinforced on promises kept. The reason most alcoholics are not trusted is that they do not keep promises. They don't because they themselves do not feel they have the emotional wherewithal and perserverance to keep them. Therefore, they have an acute need to convince others that they can and want to. This is probably why they are so fluent and persuasive. Indeed when making their promises their words, their emotional tones, and their body language all seem to be well integrated. Such an integration crumbles the family members instinct not to believe, replaces it with a positive urgency to believe. The urgency that is felt springs from the alcoholic's need to have the promise accepted. **Sophisticated non-drinking family members do not let alcoholics believe that they accept their promises.** If they do, they are enabling. For in accepting the promise they feed into the alcoholics' dilusional system that acceptance of a promise is proof that it will be fulfilled. Whether finally it is or is not fulfilled is not the issue with the alcoholic but only that it is accepted. To the alcoholic, as to anybody else, acceptance of a promise communicates trust. The rub with the alcoholic comes in fulfillment of the promise which they are unable to do and the importance of which they conveniently deny. Therefore, you **do not accept the alcoholic's promise.** Instead you confront the alcoholic with words or action that communicates, "I like your words, but what I need is action."

## Don't Let The Alcoholic Avoid Responsibilities

The final and most important point to note here is that as you do not let the alcoholic believe that you accept his/her promises, you also **do not let the alcoholics avoid responsibility.** You can and must help the alcoholic learn how to accept the responsibility of commitment and obligation. An enabler's love is misguided precisely because it lets alcoholics avoid responsibility not only in fulfilling promises but in the rest of their lives too. You can help the alcoholic by assisting him/her in doing behaviors that will lead to achieving what is meaningful. Help him/her to set goals, small ones, realistic ones and help the alcoholic to realize he/she must work on the behaviors, step by step, if he/she wants your help. You will support, you will help, you will work with him/her if steps, ever so small, are taken. In this way, you communicate that you function on positive action not positive promises.

Such behavior is particularly needed among those enablers who see themselves as practical and realistic. These people do not deny the alcoholic's disease, but see themselves as facing it squarely. They decide to cure it themselves or to help the alcoholic overcome it. In the process of curing or helping they gradually take over the alcoholic's life. Such enablers can and often do become very aggressive in this take over. They hide bottles, water down the liquor, or pour it away all together. One enabler told me that she bought her alcoholic husband's beer because, if he bought it, he'd also buy several nips. When she bought the six pack, she'd leave three cans in the car. She did this, she explained, to help him control his drinking. She firmly believed that, if only three cans were available, he'd be more likely to curb his drinking.

## Don't Control Liquor Consumed

If you and other family members do not want to enable, then **do not attempt to control the amount of liquor which the alcoholic consumes.** Moreover, such behavior doesn't work but only begets anger and feeds the alcoholics' paranoia. It reinforces their view that they can trust no one (not even family). Such behavior by enablers also engenders in alcoholics new and "creative" ways to get the liquor into the house and to find hiding places for it.

### Don't Nag, Moralize, Scold, or Blame

As they proceed in these secretive hiding ventures, they become hardened in their paranoia, in their sense that they live among enemies, that their lives are spent living in a world where it's basically "them against me." This perception is precisely what makes the alcoholic's interactions cooler, more distant, and, which in turn, begets negative reactions from enablers such as nagging, moralizing, scolding, or blaming. Therefore, you and other family members, if you seek to enhance, then **do not nag, moralize, scold, or blame.** These behaviors only alienate and harden the alcoholic's view that it's a "them against me world."

### Don't Relate In A Submissive Fashion

Some enablers are also submissive. They let the alcoholic dominate all their interactions. Such enablers are characterized by acute feelings of unworthiness. Basically they feel, just as alcoholics do, that they have little or nothing to offer anyone. They are convinced that if the alcoholic (spouse, child or parent) left there would never be another person who would be willing to stay with them. Their terror, conscious or unconscious, is that they would be left alone. To insure against such a likelihood they not only provide a veritable womb-like environment for the alcoholic but they submit to any and all demands made. The irony of the submissive-type enablers is that ultimately they are indeed left alone. Alcoholics in such emotionally crippling relationships often drink themselves to death. If they do stop drinking, they invariably leave because they recognize that their alcoholism was in some measure related to the enabler's need to keep them dependent. They recognize too that in such an environment rehabilitation is something more than difficult. Therefore, often the alcoholic is the one who leaves. The point is that if you and other family members want to promote good health in the family, then **do not relate in a submissive fashion.**

Nevertheless, some enablers submit not only to domination but even to abuse. One enabler whom I had as a client in counseling was married to a man who beat her periodically. She told me that she developed ways to encourage his abuse. She did because when her husband sobered up he felt incredibly guilty. Indeed, his guilt was such that she could ask and get the list of items she had compiled since the previous abusive incident. Once after these episodes she asked for a new car and got it. I'm convinced that these presents by the husband ultimately precipitated much anger in him because they were made out of guilt and not out of any loving choice. Not unsurprisingly, the marriage ended in divorce.

# ABOUT
# THE
# AUTHOR

Joseph F. Perez is a psychologist, Ph.D., University of Connecticut. His counseling and research with alcoholics began in 1961 at the Veterans Administration Hospital in Northampton, Massachusetts, and continues today in the college setting and in private practice.

Professor and Chairman, Department of Psychology at Westfield State College, Dr. Perez conducts seminars at the undergraduate and graduate levels on the dynamics of alcoholism and directs workshops for in-service professionals on techniques of counseling the alcoholic.

His work with the courageous people who cope with this insidious disease has led him to begin work on a book about the ironies and the anxieties engendered in the caring person. *Coping in the Alcoholic Family* is the author's eleventh professional book. Among his credits he also has a novel, *A Father's Love.*

On the lighter and personal side, Joe Perez loves college teaching because it affords him time for writing, which he describes as a "productive addiction." His other addictions, to which he freely admits, include scrabble, tennis, cooking (soups, squid, and tripe), and the New York Yankees.

He lives with his wife of thirty-two years and Mimi the youngest of their four children in Northampton, Massachusetts.